FAMOUS GUNFIGHTS OF TEXAS

by Dave Southworth

Cover design by Chip Southworth

Library of Congress Cataloging-In-Publication Data
Library of Congress Control Number: 2010922956

Southworth, Dave
Famous Gunfights of Texas

    Bibliography: p. 155
    Index: p.163

1. Texas—History—Biography. 2. Outlaws—Texas—Biography.
3. Lawmen—Texas—Biography. 4. West (U.S.)—History—Biography.
5. Outlaws—West (U.S.)—Biography. 6. Lawmen—West (U.S.)—Biography. 7. West (U.S.)—History—Sources. 8. Frontier and Pioneer Life—West (U.S.)—Sources.

ISBN: 978-1-890778-14-9
      1-890778-14-1

Copyright: 2010 by Dave Southworth
Printed in the United States of America

All rights reserved. Without limiting the rights under copyright reserved above, no part of this book may be reproduced, stored in or introduced into a retrieval system, or transmitted, in any form or by any means (electronically, mechanically, by photocopying, recording or otherwise) without the written permission of the copyright owner.

Contents

Preface			Page	5
Chapter	1	The Battle of Dry Creek	Page	9
Chapter	2	Jim Courtright and Luke Short	Page	13
Chapter	3	John Wesley Hardin: Deadly Son of a Preacher	Page	19
Chapter	4	Feuds of the Horrell Clan	Page	25
Chapter	5	Bad, Bad Clay Allison	Page	39
Chapter	6	Shootout at Round Rock	Page	41
Chapter	7	The Lee-Peacock Feud	Page	45
Chapter	8	Dee Harkey: Guts and Grit	Page	49
Chapter	9	The Jaybird-Woodpecker Conflict	Page	55
Chapter	10	The Hoodoo War	Page	61
Chapter	11	Bulletproof Killer and the Pecos Grudge	Page	67
Chapater	12	The Sutton-Taylor Feud	Page	69
Chapter	13	Cullen Baker: Fugitive	Page	93
Chapter	14	He'll Hang Again and Again!	Page	95
Chapter	15	Vaudeville and Vengeance	Page	97
Chapter	16	El Paso's Fighting Marshal	Page	103
Chapter	17	Reprisal in Bell County	Page	107
Chapter	18	The Mitchell-Truitt Conflict	Page	111
Chapter	19	Shootout on Christmas Day	Page	115
Chapter	20	Orator, Lawyer, Sharp-Shooter	Page	121
Chapter	21	Laredo: The Botas and Guaraches	Page	129
Chapter	22	The Corps of Rangers	Page	133
Chapter	23	Ira Aten: Lawman	Page	137
Chapter	24	Albert Jennings Fountain	Page	141
Chapter	25	The Law West of the Pecos	Page	145
Chapter	26	Guns and Gunmakers	Page	147
Bibliography			Page	155
Index			Page	163

WORKS BY DAVE SOUTHWORTH

BOOKS: NON-FICTION

Famous Gunfights of the American West
Feuds on the Western Frontier
Colorado Gold Dust: Short Stories and Profiles
Colorado Mining Camps
Ghost Towns and Mining Camps of the San Juans
Gunfighters of the Old West
Gunfighters of the Old West II
Famous Gunfights of Texas
Leadville

BOOKS: FICTION

Franklin Hall
Rhymes of a Storyteller

VIDEOS

Colorado Mining Camps: A Pictorial Treasure of the
    Gold and Silver Boom
Leadville: The Boom Years
Mining Camps of the San Juans
Cripple Creek and the Mining Camps of Teller County
The Mining Camps of Northwest Colorado
Boulder County Mining Camps: A Look Back
The Mining Camps of Gilpin and Clear Creek Counties
The Mining Camps of South Central Colorado

AUDIO BOOKS

Gunfighters of the Old West
Colorado Gold Dust: Short Stories and Profiles
Billy the Kid and the Lincoln County War
Jesse James and the James-Younger Gang
Doc Holliday and the Earp Brothers

O bury me not on the lone prairie,
Where the wild coyotes will howl o'er me,
In a narrow grave just six by three,
O bury me not on the lone prairie …

Gunfights in early Texas and throughout the American West usually resulted because of mutual hostility between two or more individuals, clans, tribes, families or other groups. Or, they occurred because one party infringed upon the rights and property of the other, as was the case when a robbery, or attempted robbery, took place. Sometimes the gunfights were spontaneous. Sometimes they occurred because of prolonged hostilities between the parties involved. Often they were marked by murderous assaults in revenge for some previous insult or injustice. In many cases a quarrel would intensify, as ill will and animosity increased, until both parties engaged in battle. Basically, each participant strived for satisfaction or gratification for what they thought was some unjust deed. That deed could have been something as simple as an insult, or an offense to one's honor or pride. Many gunfights erupted due to a seemingly insignificant incident. Conversely, its origin can sometimes be traced to an episode of serious magnitude. There were feuds that lasted for months, even years, during which many confrontations might occur. The roots of such feuds took many forms. There were disputes over land rights or claim rights; conflicts between political parties; clashes with ethnic overtones; discord between large and small cattle ranchers; hostilities between cattlemen and sheep herders; and labor wars.

At the root of each conflict are two or more people, with different opinions, certain that they are right and their opposition wrong. Common sense, litigation and mediators usually did little to resolve unwavering differences. Guns were often the last resort. Actually, they were sometimes the first resort as well. Indifferences that have become historically prominent usually have done so because of their gunfights and bloodshed. Animosity, from whatever the cause, would usually grow and then blossom to its fullest. Rarely would it simply wilt and die. Sometimes it had to be cut off by intervention of a third party of greater strength, or by mutual extermination.

"An eye for an eye and a tooth for a tooth" is the oldest code of law enforcement known to man. It was also the code of revenge and retribution across much of the early Western Frontier. To what degree could one consider lawless the act of "taking the law into one's own hands" especially in places where reasonable legal redress could not be obtained? To arm one's family or group, or to establish a committee of vigilance for the purpose of self-preservation, did not necessarily constitute disrespect for the law. The disrespect occurred when the individuals, feudists or vigilantes overplayed their role as "frontier lawmen." Usually when men take the law into their own hands, they do so until they commit atrocities under the guise of doing what is "lawful." Hostilities developed with different scenarios—with both factions believing they had the right to be lawmen, judge and jury.

Conflicts have occurred around the world, throughout recorded history. There were many in early Texas. This book presents some of the more significant encounters during the post-Civil War period (from about 1865 until shortly after the turn of the century). Most of the gunfights that appear here occurred within the boundaries of Texas. Those that did not are mentioned because of their importance to the story of the Texan(s) involved. During the years of the great cattle drives, tired Texas cowboys created trouble in many railhead destinations. Drovers spent long days in the saddle, struggling through dust storms and rain storms, facing the fear of Indian attacks or rustlers and the terror of night lightning sparking a stampede. Once they loaded their stock into the chutes and received their pay, they were more than ready to play. They would shoot up a town, ride their horses into saloons, find the nearest brothel, pour plenty of whiskey down the hatch, and be just as disorderly as possible. Many wound up in confrontations of one kind or another, either with the law or with locals the drovers may have insulted. Some would attempt to refight the Civil War. Many wound up in jail. Some wound up dead. There were many gunfights outside of the state of Texas that involved Texans. With a few exceptions their stories are not told here. One feud of note broke out years before the Civil War—the Regulator-Moderator War which occurred in and around Shelby County from 1839 to 1844. This, along with the Battle of the Alamo, the raids of Mexican Juan Cortinas in the late 1850s, episodes in the Mexican War, and Civil War events are also not included here. Furthermore, the stories of the mobs in San Saba and Shackelford counties are excluded as well. Those are happenings that the folks in those areas would like to forget, so they are not retold here. There were hundreds of gunfights in the post-Civil War period of the nineteenth century alone.

The gunfights which unfold throughout the following pages were selected for inclusion based on interest, renown, variety and/or historical significance. Many of the participants are individuals of much notoriety. The cast of characters includes John Wesley Hardin, "Deacon" Jim Miller, Jim Courtright, Luke Short, Sam Bass and Bill Longley. Much of the action, however, is, and was, created by those with lesser reputations.

Temple Houston and Albert Jennings Fountain were not known as gunfighters. Both were involved in gunfights, however, and their interesting stories are included here. Also, no book on the Old West in Texas is complete without mentioning Judge Roy Bean, the "Law West of the Pecos."

There is no order to the following chapters, either chronological or geographical. The author has also attempted to present the workings of frontier justice in many of these conflicts strictly as historical events without any bias or judgment toward any faction involved. There were always two sides to every story.

Charles (left) and George Marlow, while shackled to two dead brothers, fought off a mob intent on lynching them. *Marlow Chamber of Commerce, Courtesy of the Marlow Family.*

Chapter One
The Battle at Dry Creek

George, Charles, Boone, Alfred "Alf," and Lewellyn "Ep" Marlow were brothers. They were sons of Martha Jane and Dr. Wilson Williamson Marlow. Ep was the youngest of the five. The brothers were a courageous and gutsy bunch, and were involved in one of the most amazing gunfights in Texas history.

On April 15, 1886, the year after Dr. Marlow's death, Boone killed a man near Vernon, in Wilbarger County, Texas. Although Boone claimed to have never seen James H. Holston before, it may be that Holston had been carrying an old grudge against Boone. When Holston decided to rid the country of Boone Marlow he made a grave mistake. Holston took Boone by surprise as he was approaching his sister's house, and opened fire on him. Boone grabbed his Winchester and returned the fire with much greater accuracy. James Holston fell dead. Suddenly Boone was a wanted man. The brothers headed to Colorado with the hope that things would cool down.

Two years later they decided that enough time had passed, and that it would be safe to return to the Southwest. They were wrong. The five brothers were arrested for stealing horses in Indian Territory and jailed in Graham, Texas. The charge was later proven to be unfounded. After being freed on bail, they went to live at the O. G. Denson farm in Young County, about 12 miles (19 kilometers) from Graham. Shortly before Christmas, on December 16, 1888, Sheriff Marion DeKalb Wallace and Deputy Sheriff Thomas B. "Tom" Collier rode to the Denson farm with a warrant for the arrest of Boone Marlow in connection with the 1886 murder of James Holston in Wilbarger County. Collier was the first to enter the house. He drew his pistol and fired the first shot. Boone grabbed his Winchester and shot back. His first bullet went through the deputy's hat, and the second struck Wallace as he approached the front door. Boone ran to the door as Wallace tumbled outside on the porch floor. Both of his kidneys were damaged and Sheriff M. D. Wallace died a week later. Boone suddenly had a price on his head. The governor posted a reward of $200 for Boone Marlow dead or alive. Citizens of Young County added another $1,500 making the total reward $1,700. Feeling the heat, Boone fled the area.

Near a spot called Hell Creek in Indian Territory, twenty miles (32 kilometers) from Fort Sill, Oklahoma, Boone hid out at the place of his ex-sweetheart, Susan Harbolt. The bounty on Boone's head was attractive to Susan's brother, George E. Harbolt, and two cohorts Jim Beavers and John E. Derrickson. They evidently poisoned Marlow and then shot him before carrying his body to Fort Sill and then on to Graham for the reward. After receiving their reward the trio was later arrested and charged with murder. When he died on January 28, 1889,

The five Marlow brothers, (from Left to Right) George, Boone, Alfred, Lewellyn and Charles. *Marlow Chamber of Commerce, Courtesy of the Marlow Family.*

Boone Marlow never knew the fate of his brothers who were involved in an incredible shootout nine days earlier in Texas.

After Boone fled to Oklahoma, Charles, Alf, and Ep Marlow were arrested for complicity in the shooting of Marion Wallace. Ep actually rode to Graham, Texas, to get a physician for Wallace after the shooting occurred. He was arrested and jailed before he could leave town. Charles and Alf were arrested and transported to Graham to stand trial in federal court. When George (and other family members) went to Graham in an effort to clear his brothers, he was also jailed. The citizens of Graham were mad that their sheriff had been killed and they wanted revenge. The Marlows escaped from the jailhouse on January 14, 1889, but were caught and returned to their cell the following morning.

An unruly mob, all masked, wanted to lynch the Marlow brothers and they surrounded the jail on the night of January 17, 1889, but they had no success. They were afraid to fire a shot as it might waken the townspeople, and the prisoners were able to repel the mob with one mighty punch thrown by Charles Marlow, and a piece of water pipe. Charles Marlow's punch knocked the unidentified man unconscious. He was dragged from the scene. Whether by coincidence, or not, one of the local citizens who was in fine health the morning of the 17th, died within a couple of days from "brain fever." Tom Collier, the new sheriff, and others concocted a story that an attempt was made by Boone Marlow and a large group of men to break the prisoners out of jail, but that the effort was resisted by local lawmen. Upon hearing this fabrication at his office in Dallas, Deputy U. S. Marshal Ben F. Cabell ordered the prisoners moved to a safer jailhouse in Weatherford, Texas.

Graham peace officers, in cahoots with the mob, decided that it was time to act again. After dark, on January 19, 1889, the Marlows were put in irons for the trip to Weatherford. George was shackled to Ep, and Charles was shackled to Alf. Two other prisoners, William D. Burkhart and Louis Clift were shackled to each other. There were seven guards, six who were armed, while the driver of the hack carrying the prisoners was not. There was another hack and a buggy in which the armed guards rode. As the group reached Dry Creek, outside of Graham, all hell broke loose. It was approximately 9 p.m. The mob, all masked, had been waiting, and they opened fire. Although shackled together, Alf and Charles jumped over the side of their hack and quickly got to the guards' hack. George and Ep did the same. Alf grabbed somebody's gun barrel, and in the process was riddled by bullets. Meanwhile, the other prisoners were able to wrestle guns away from the guards and turned them on the mob. One guard was killed and two were injured. The prisoners also grabbed the weapons of the fallen guards. The remaining guards ran to escape the barrage of bullets and to join the mob. Ep was blown to shreds by the mob's gunfire. He was dead. His body was so mutilated that it later needed to be bound up with strips of cloth so he could be dressed for his casket. George had been shot in one hand. Charles had been shot in the jaw and the chest. Louis Clift took a slug in one leg. While shackled to their two dead brothers, George and Charles continued to shoot at the mob. The astonished mob retreated into the woods to reorganize. With a knife that was taken from one of the bodies, Charles was able to separate himself from Alf by cutting off his foot. He then came to the aid of George who couldn't handle the knife because of the wound to his hand. Charles proceeded to amputate Ep's foot in order to free George. Charles, George, Burkhart, and Clift climbed into one of the wagons and with Burkhart driving they fled from the scene. The mob was so stunned that it gave no effort to pursue the wagon. They had planned on a "peaceful" lynching, not a gunfight. The guard that was killed, Sam Criswell, was one of the mob's conspirators. The other two riders in the mob that were shot and killed were, Bruce Wheeler and Frank Harmeson. Both were instigators in the mob action. In addition to all the deaths, and the wounds to George, Charles, and Louis Clift, at least three other men had been shot, and the wounded may have totaled five.

The two Marlow brothers headed back to the Denson farm where they agreed to surrender to Deputy U. S. Marshal W. H. Morton who assured them protection. They were taken to Dallas where they were tried and acquitted. After George and Charles were exonerated of any wrongdoing, they both moved to Colorado where they became peace officers and prominent citizens. Charles died in California on January 19, 1941, fifty-two years to the day after the battle at Dry Creek. George died July 3, 1945 in Colorado.

In 1891, several members of the mob were sentenced for their part in the attack on the Marlows. The battle at Dry Creek was extraordinary. It was the only time in the annals of recorded history that unarmed men shackled together were able through amazing courage and guts to hold off a mob intent on lynching them.

Gambler Luke Short carried his six-shooter in a leather lined pants pocket. *Kansas State Historical Society.*

Chapter Two
Jim Courtright and Luke Short

Timothy Isaiah Courtright was born in the year 1845 at Abraham Lincoln's hometown, Springfield, Illinois. He was one of six children raised in a strict farming family. Courtright left home when he was fifteen and worked his way to Iowa. At the age of sixteen, he enlisted in an Iowa regiment of the Union Army, and fought under General John "Blackjack" Logan during the Civil War. Somehow, about this time, Tim became Jim, and the lad who wore his hair long was dubbed "Longhaired Jim".

General Logan took a special interest in Courtright, possibly because of his accurate marksmanship. Jim was Logan's most trusted scout, and the two cultivated a friendship which would last long after the war was over.

After the Confederate States surrendered, Courtright was stationed in Missouri with another Union scout, Wild Bill Hickok. Longhaired Jim was then transferred to Little Rock, Arkansas, where he met the love of his life, Sarah Elizabeth (Betty) Weeks. Betty, a mature fourteen-year-old, and Jim were married in 1866 following a short courtship. Jim trained Betty in the art of firearms, and she became an excellent marksman, as well. For a while the couple performed a shooting act with a touring Wild West show.

On April 5, 1876, Jim Courtright was appointed city marshal of Fort Worth, Texas. Longhaired Jim (whose long hair was now gone) performed his duties well as an officer of the law, but became too involved in the political scene. He backed the wrong party and it cost him his position as marshal.

Following a friend's recommendation, Courtright accepted a position as security guard for the American Mining Company in the booming new silver camp at Lake Valley, New Mexico. One night while Jim was on duty, two Mexican outlaws attempted to rob a shipment of ore. It was their last mistake. In the gunfight which ensued, both bandits were slain by the accurate rifle shots of Jim Courtright.

Before long, the mines played out and the population of Lake Valley dwindled. In need of employment once again, Jim contacted his old friend and former commanding officer General John Logan who owned a cattle ranch near Silver City, New Mexico. Logan's ranch had been plagued by cattle rustlers and unwanted nesters (squatters), so the timing was perfect to employ Courtright's keen marksmanship. Jim was hired by Logan as a ranch foreman.

One afternoon in 1883, Jim Courtright and Jim McIntire rode out to the shack of two French squatters, to see if they had responded to a previous order to get off the property. The Frenchmen had ignored the warning. McIntire (who was also a former city marshal) and Courtright shot and killed the nesters. Throughout the vicinity an outcry arose over the slayings. Courtright and McIntire decided to flee the area. Longhaired Jim headed back to Fort Worth where he assumed he would be safe. Meanwhile, warrants had been issued in New Mexico for the arrest of both Jims on the charge of murder. The following year, Courtright was surprised when (on October 18, 1884) he was placed under arrest by a relentless New Mexico lawman, John Richmond, and two Texas Rangers.

On the day after Courtright's arrest, officers escorted him to a nearby restaurant for a meal. A mob entered the restaurant and closed in around Courtright's table. During the confusion, he dropped a napkin, leaned over to pick it up and somehow came up with two revolvers which he quickly pointed at the lawmen. The officers had no choice but to back away and watch Courtright escape.

Over a period of time, the folks around Silver City, New Mexico, had virtually forgotten about the deaths of the two Frenchmen. Eventually, both McIntire and Courtright returned to Silver City and turned themselves in. By then, the outraged nesters had moved on, and the influence of General Logan on the townspeople led to rapid acquittals for each.

Once again Jim returned to Fort Worth where he established the T.I.C. Commercial Detective Agency, with Jim McIntire as a partner. The agency primarily operated a protection racket. T.I.C. (the initials of Courtright's given name) "protected" gambling joints and gamblers in return for a monthly fee. One gambler who refused to participate in Courtright's shakedown was cool and dapper Luke Short of Dodge City fame.

Luke Lamar Short was born in Mississippi, in 1854. His family moved to Texas when Luke was only two-years-old. As a teenager he worked as a drover to trail cattle herds to the Kansas railheads. Seeking a more lucrative existence, he headed to Nebraska and began peddling bootleg whiskey to the Sioux Indians. His business thrived until he was arrested by the U. S. Army. Shortly thereafter, Luke headed to the silver camp at Leadville, Colorado. There he operated as a professional gambler. It was a trade he would practice for the rest of his life. Eventually, he showed up in Dodge City, Kansas, where he purchased the gaming concession at the Long Branch Saloon. During his time in Dodge City, Short became fast friends with Bat Masterson and Wyatt Earp. Later he traveled to Tombstone, Arizona, where he dealt faro at the Oriental Saloon. Nearly twelve years after he first arrived in Dodge City, Luke Short returned with money in his pocket. He purchased the Long Branch Saloon which he operated for about four years, before moving on to Ft. Worth, Texas. There, Luke and his partner, Jake Johnson, owned the gaming concession at the White Elephant Saloon.

Evidently, the T.I.C. Commercial Detective Agency had sent Luke Short a threatening note. Short and his friend Bat Masterson set out to find Courtright. When they did, the ensuing confrontation didn't last long. As heated words were exchanged, Short reached inside his coat. Believing that Short was going for his gun, the fast and usually deadly Courtright drew and squeezed his trigger. His revolver didn't discharge. The delay gave Short (who carried his revolver in a specially tailored leather-lined pocket) time to draw and fire. By fate, or luck, Short's first bullet struck the cylinder of Courtright's revolver making it useless. Short emptied his pistol, with three slugs hitting Courtright in the right shoulder, right thumb and heart. Officer J.J. Fulford arrived at the scene immediately to find his friend lying on his back. Courtright mumbled his last words, "Ful, they've got me."

The crowd that quickly gathered was astonished. Jim Courtright was fast and accurate, and seemingly invincible in a gunfight. People were amazed that Luke Short (who carried his revolver in a pocket)

Jim Courtright was a deadly marksman. He once killed four men in two gunfights. *Wild Horse Collection.*

could come out victorious against such a formidable foe. Luke Short was lucky. It is believed that when Courtright first squeezed his trigger the hammer caught on his watch chain. That, and the fact that Short's first bullet struck the cylinder of Courtright's revolver, made this a most bizarre gunfight.

The gunfight precipitated much controversy. Some say it wasn't the watch chain which prevented Courtright's pistol from discharging—and that the cylinder had actually jammed. This seems unlikely as Courtright would have kept his weapons in fine working condition. Others believe that Short's first shot hit Courtright's thumb making him unable to cock his hammer. The general consensus is that Courtright won the draw, and that his weapon misfired.

Longhaired Jim Courtright was buried at Pioneer's Rest Cemetery. His body was later moved to the Oakwood Cemetery at Fort Worth. After Jim's death, Betty Courtright moved to California.

Luke Short was never convicted in the slaying of Jim Courtright. On December 23, 1890, Short was wounded in a gunfight following an argument with another gambler named Charles Wright. Wright ambushed Short with a shotgun blast from behind. Some of the buckshot hit Luke's left leg. Short returned fire with one of his bullets striking Wright's wrist before he was able to scamper to safety. Later, Short suffered from edema (or dropsy), and his health worsened. Luke went to the mineral spa at Geuda Springs, Kansas, for therapy. While there, Luke Short died on September 8, 1893. His remains also lie in the Oakwood Cemetery at Ft. Worth.

The Courtright-Short gunfight, that occurred on February 8, 1887, may be the most famous confrontation between two such formidable and celebrated individuals in the annals of Old West history.

18

John Wesley Hardin in 1871 at the age of 18. When this photograph was taken in Abilene, Hardin was already a seasoned gunfighter. *Kansas State Historical Society.*

Chapter Three
John Wesley Hardin: Deadly Son of a Preacher

John Wesley Hardin was born in Bonham, Texas, on May 26, 1853, and named for the founder of the Methodist faith. Wes, as he was usually called, was the son of Mary Elizabeth Hardin and James Hardin, a circuit preacher of the same denomination. Wes and his father were very similar in many ways, but totally different in others. Both were intelligent, and had a thirst for knowledge. Each taught school for a while, and during some point in their lives they both practiced law. But there the similarities ended. While his father spread the word of God, Wes Hardin became one of the most dangerous of all western gunmen.

In two separate incidents, during November of 1868, fifteen-year-old Wes Hardin killed his first four men. While visiting his uncle's farm near Moscow in eastern Texas, Hardin got into a scuffle with a former slave named Mage. After Mage got his nose bloodied, he threatened Wes. The following day, as he was riding back to the farm, Hardin was accosted by Mage who was carrying a big stick. The former slave seized the bridle of Wes' horse. Hardin drew his revolver and shot the man three times. Mage died within days. Wes headed home to tell his father about the incident. Fearing carpetbagger justice, the elder Hardin suggested that Wes lay low for a while. He traveled northeast to a friend's farm, believed to be near Sumner, to hide out. While he was there, he received word from his brother Joseph that Union soldiers were in the vicinity looking for him. He knew that if the soldiers headed toward the farm, they would need to slow down at a nearby creek crossing, so he set up camp there and waited. Before long three bluecoats approached. Hardin ambushed the soldiers as they crossed the creek, killing two with blasts from his double-barrel shotgun. The other soldier drew, and returned fire grazing Hardin's left arm. By then, Wes had drawn his revolver and gunned down the third soldier.

The Hardins had relatives and friends throughout central Texas who were glad to shelter the fugitive from "Yankee avengers." So, Wes fled south to Navarro County where he stayed with relatives and worked for a short time as a school teacher, and then as a cowhand. Wes then ventured further south, and trouble followed him. One evening, Hardin was approached by a fellow whom he had beaten badly in a card game earlier in the day. The poor loser fired a shot at Hardin. It was the last thing he ever did, as Hardin dropped him with a slug in the head, and another in the chest. Within days, Wes Hardin shot down an employee of a circus troupe following a quarrel. He then fled to another uncle's farm, near Brenham, where he would lay low for a few months.

Not wanting to stay in any one place too long, Hardin decided to head for Louisiana. Before he reached the state line, he was arrested by a deputy sheriff near the town of Marshall. He was charged with a murder that had occurred in Waco, which he had not committed. While captive in the small jailhouse at Marshall, Hardin somehow obtained a Colt revolver, which he kept hidden. A Captain Stokes, of the newly organized and short-lived Texas State Police, and a guard named Jim Smolly, were assigned the duty of transporting Hardin from Marshall to Waco for trial. During their trip west, Stokes left Smolly to guard Hardin while he went to a nearby farmhouse to find some fodder for the horses. It was the advantage Hardin was looking for. He produced the revolver that he had kept hidden and mortally wounded Smolly. He quickly mounted and fled the scene before Stokes returned.

Wes Hardin headed to Gonzales County and the cattle ranch of his cousins, the Clements, south of the town of Smiley. There he worked as a cowpoke and found safety for a while. A cattle drive carried him to

Abilene, Kansas, during the summer of 1871, where he dispatched a fellow named Charles Cougar, following a quarrel.

The very next day, Wes Hardin joined a manhunt for a Mexican named Juan Bideno. Wes was joined by Hugh Anderson, Jim Rodgers, and John Cohron, whose brother Bill had been killed by Bideno two days earlier. The group tracked the Mexican to the settlement of Bluff City, about five miles (8 kilometers) north of the Oklahoma state line, where they found him eating at a café. As Hardin walked in, with the others behind him, Wes shot Bideno through the head at close range.

During his brief stay in Kansas, John Wesley Hardin was supposedly befriended by Wild Bill Hickok, who was city marshal of Abilene at the time. Upon completion of their business, Hardin and the other cowhands returned to Texas and the Clements' cattle ranch. He hadn't been back long when he heard that two members of the Texas State Police were asking questions about him in Smiley. Hardin, apparently intent on a fight, sought the duo out. He approached them as they were eating crackers at the general store. According to the popular version of the story, Wes asked the policemen who they were looking for. After they responded, he asked if they would recognize Hardin when they saw him. One of the officers replied that they had never seen him. "Well," said Hardin, "you see him now!" As he spoke he drew and fatally shot Green Parramore in the head. His second shot hit John Lackey in the mouth and he reeled backwards. Lackey was able to scramble out the front door and run for cover. Cautiously, Hardin exited through the rear door and rounded the building only to find that Lackey had disappeared. Unbeknownst to Hardin, the policeman had fled to nearby Round Lake where he submerged himself. The cold water helped curtail the bleeding, and Lackey survived.

Hoping to settle down one day, Wes Hardin married his longtime sweetheart, Jane Bowen. Wes once said of her, "She was as true to me as the magnet of steel." During their marriage, Jane gave birth to three children, two daughters and a son. When he was traveling Hardin had been known to ride a long distance to see Jane. On one occasion, he covered about a hundred miles (62 kilometers) in six hours. Commenting about the trip, in his own words, Hardin said, "…ruined a good horse worth $50 doing so. The sight of my wife recompensed me for the loss of old Bob."

During the year 1872, Wes Hardin was involved in shootings in Sabine, Trinity, and Angelina counties. He was wounded twice, and was also captured. Mannen Clements broke Hardin out of jail in October of that year. Clements slipped a file to Wes, with which he cut the bars. Mannen then returned and pulled Hardin through the opening with his lariat. Wes then joined his cousins in the Sutton-Taylor feud.

They fought for the Taylor clan. The Taylors and Clements were related by marriage. In one incident, Hardin and Jim Taylor were confronted by Jack Helm who fought for the Sutton faction. He was accompanied by six cohorts. Hardin raised his shotgun and blasted Helm in the chest. After he collapsed, Taylor fired several rounds into the dying man's head. When the action started, Helm's cohorts quickly scampered away.

Comanche, Texas, was the scene of the killing for which John Wesley Hardin was eventually convicted and imprisoned. It was May 26, 1874 (Hardin's twenty-first birthday) and the town was festive with people who had gathered for horse races. Wes had won a substantial amount of money on the races, but his day was dampened when he learned that Charles Webb, deputy sheriff of nearby Brown County was in town with the intention of killing Hardin. Webb found Hardin at Jack Wright's Saloon. Hardin invited Webb to the bar for a drink As Webb stepped toward the bar, he drew his revolver and fired. Hardin was alert and jumped to one side and the deputy's shot only grazed him. Wes fired, and his bullet hit Webb in the head. The deputy sheriff collapsed on the barroom floor. He was dead. Wes, his cousin Bill Dixon, and Jim Taylor, who had accompanied him to the bar, all fled. Not able to find Wes and his companions, an enraged mob from Brown County sought out Wes's brother, Joseph Hardin, and cousins Joe and Bud Dixon, and then lynched them all. John Wesley Hardin had a $4,000 price on his head, and he felt the heat. Wes and his wife Jane left the state.

For three years in Florida and Alabama, Wes remained anonymous under the alias of J. H. Swain, Jr. during which time he brokered cattle and horses and dabbled in other businesses. The Texas Rangers finally discovered his whereabouts, and cornered Hardin while he was on a business trip in Pensacola, Florida. While Hardin's train sat at the depot, John Armstrong and other Texas Rangers stormed both ends of the smoking car where Wes was relaxing with friends. Hardin reached for a concealed revolver, but as he drew the weapon caught on his suspenders. Jim Mann, who was sitting beside Wes, drew his pistol and fired at Armstrong. As the bullet sailed harmlessly through the ranger's hat, Armstrong put a fatal shot into Mann's chest. Armstrong then slugged Hardin with the barrel of his revolver and took the fugitive into custody. Hardin was tried in Austin, Texas, and was found guilty of second-degree murder for the slaying of Deputy Sheriff Charles Webb. John Wesley Hardin was sentenced to a term of twenty-five years in the penitentiary at Huntsville.

Wes Hardin spent his years in prison constructively. He studied law. After serving fifteen years, Hardin was released in February of 1894, and pardoned the following month. His wife Jane had died two years earlier. Wes went to Gonzales where he opened a law practice and lived for a while with his children. He soon moved his law practice to Junction and then on to El Paso. It was during this time that he penned his autobiography, *The Life of John Wesley Hardin as Written by Himself*. While residing in Junction, Wes married a young girl named Callie Lewis. Within hours after their vows were exchanged, Callie packed up and left him. The despondent Wes Hardin relocated to Kerr County where he stayed briefly before moving on to El Paso.

Wes Hardin reopened his law practice in his room on the second floor of the Herndon Lodging House. Actually, it was a case that brought Hardin to El Paso in the first place. His services had been procured by notorious gunman "Deacon" Jim Miller, who earlier had married Sallie Clements, daughter of Mannen. Hardin was hired by Miller to prosecute a man who had tried to kill him. Wes didn't have many other clients, however, and business was slow. He spent many hours at either the Acme Saloon or whoring around with Helen Buelah Morose, a former prostitute and wife of rustler Martin Morose. Speculation has it that Wes Hardin and John Selman, city constable, conspired to kill Martin Morose. Morose's death would benefit both. Selman would be rid of a nemesis, and an obstacle would be eliminated in Hardin's romance with Buelah Morose. At any rate, Martin Morose turned up dead. According to rumor, he had a large sum of money in his possession when he was slain, and furthermore that Hardin grabbed the money and failed to split it with Selman. Whether this was just a rumor or whether this precipitated Selman's actions of August 19, 1895, we may never know.

On that date, during the evening, Wes Hardin was in the Acme Saloon, rolling dice on the bar top with an acquaintance. John Selman entered the saloon and began shooting—at Hardin's back. Wes Hardin never had a chance to draw. As his lifeless body crumpled to the floor Selman continued to shoot until he was restrained by his son, John Selman, Jr., and Chief Jeff Milton, both members of the El Paso police force.

The incident was so clouded by conflicting testimony that a hung jury was the result. A retrial was scheduled, but John Selman was gunned down by Deputy U. S. Marshal, George Scarborough, before the case came to court.

There were other explanations as to Selman's motive in the Acme Saloon slaying of Hardin. Some say he was simply after the acclaim for disposing of such a famed gunfighter as John Wesley Hardin, and adding another notch to a list that already included a Deputy U. S. Marshal, Bass Outlaw, among others.

John Wesley Hardin was probably involved in more gunfights than anyone else on the western frontier. No one will ever know just how many men he actually killed. He claimed to have disposed of forty-four, but then again, he was known to blow a little smoke. Only about twenty-five percent of those are verifiable through county records and documents, but then again, in those days, many deaths went unrecorded. Regardless of the count, Wes Hardin, the deadly son of a preacher, was one of the most dangerous gunfighters of all.

This photograph of early Lampasas, Texas, shows the scene of a gunfight that occurred on June 7, 1877, between the feuding Horrell and Higgins factions. Looking west down Third Street, its intersection with Live Oak Street is at right and the public square at left. *Keystone Square Museum and the Lampasas County Historical Commission.*

Chapter Four
Feuds of the Horrell Clan

Trouble followed the Arkansas-born, Texas-bred Horrells wherever they went. Much of it was of their own making. "The Horrell War" occurred in Lincoln County, New Mexico, in late 1873 and early 1874. Basically it was a conflict between Tejanos (Texans) and Hispanics. "The Horrell-Higgins Feud" which occurred in Lampasas County, Texas, culminated in 1877. Both were bloody affairs.

Between 1839 and 1857 the marriage of Samuel and Elizabeth Horrell produced eight children: William, John, Samuel, Jr., James Martin "Mart", Thomas, Benjamin, Merritt, and Sarah. They were a tough bunch. The Horrell family moved from Caddo Gap, Arkansas, to a ranch near Lampasas, Texas, in about 1857. Eleven years later they packed up their belongings and set out for California with a thousand head of cattle. When they reached Las Cruces, New Mexico, they sold their herd. The oldest son, John (William is believed to have perished during the Civil War), gathered the drovers to pay them their final wages. In a dispute over the amount of his wages, a cowpoke named Early Hubbard killed John Horrell. The family decided to stay in the vicinity, at least for a while. About three months later Sam, Sr., met his demise at the hands of Apaches near the San Agustin Pass in the San Andres Mountains. Soon thereafter the Horrells pulled up stakes and returned to the Lampasas, Texas area.

John, Mart and Ben had married three sisters. Children were

born to each of the couples. Tom also married but had no offspring. Merritt, the youngest son, remained a bachelor and lived with Mart and his family. The brothers raised cattle in the area along Little Lucy Creek. They were a no-nonsense bunch, and each of the boys was very skillful with firearms. The Horrells were well liked and had many friends.

State Police Chief, F. L. Britton notified Governor Edmund Davis that action was necessary to bring a large gang of rustlers to justice and listed four of the Horrell brothers among sixteen names in his report. Shortly thereafter, two Horrell friends, G. W. and Mark Short were involved in an altercation during which G. W. Short shot the sheriff. When a posse attempted to arrest the Shorts, Ben, Tom and Mart Horrell, accompanied by a number of their cohorts, intervened with guns drawn. The posse had no alternative but to watch in vain as the Shorts rode to safety.

A law enacted in 1871 to "Regulate the Keeping and Bearing of Deadly Weapons" specifically excluded Lampasas County. The Short brothers' incident was the catalyst which prompted Governor Davis to extend the law to include Lampasas County. F. L. Britton sent seven policemen, under the command of Captain Thomas G. Williams, to Lampasas in order to enforce the new provisions.

Bill Bowen, a fugitive from the law, had fled to Lampasas months earlier to seek refuge with his in-laws, the Horrells. On March 14, 1873,

Mart Horrell was wounded in a shootout with police at Jerry Scott's Matador Saloon. *Sarah Harrison Cobb.*

Sam, Mart and Tom Horrell were having drinks at Jerry Scott's Matador Saloon with several cowboys including Bowen when they were confronted by members of the State Police. Captain Tom Williams and the other policemen had seen Bowen go into the saloon and decided to investigate. After entering the building, they tried to arrest Bowen for wearing a revolver. When Williams approached him and attempted to grab his pistol, gunfire erupted. Captain Williams and Officer T. M. Daniels were killed instantly. The lifeless body of Officer Wesley Cherry crumbled to the ground just outside the door. Another policeman, Andrew Melville, was shot in the street. He staggered into a hotel but would soon die. Three other officers were able to flee. Mart Horrell was injured in the exchange of gunfire. He was taken to his mother's home to recuperate. Within a few days a posse of policemen, headed by Britton, arrived at Elizabeth's home and arrested Mart. They also arrested Allen Whitecraft, Jim Jenkins, Jerry Scott and James Grizell. None of the others could be found. The five prisoners were jailed at Austin. Horrell and Scott were then transferred to Georgetown. Artemisa Horrell was allowed to remain with her husband, Mart, to nurse his wound.

Once Artemisa thought that Mart was capable of riding she notified his brothers. On the 2nd of May a mob of about thirty-five men rode into Georgetown in a show of force. While most of the men were shooting at random in order to keep townspeople at bay, Bill Bowen smashed in the jailhouse door with a sledgehammer. The prisoners were freed, and the mob rode off into the night. A. S. Fisher, a local attorney, was wounded by a bullet during the jailbreak.

The Horrells decided that it was time to pack up and leave Texas in search of greener pastures. After selling most of their cattle to local businessmen, the clan assembled its wagons and headed west.

In late September of 1873, the Horrells settled along the Ruidoso River, in Lincoln County, New Mexico. They probably could have picked a better spot. There had been several incidents which created friction between Hispanics and Anglos in the vicinity. In the eyes of Ruidoso Valley Hispanics, Tejanos (Texans) were as bad as Anglos could be. The feud which unfolded over the next few months was predominately between Texans and Hispanics. It is commonly referred to as "The Horrell War."

The first bloody conflict occurred on the night of December 1, 1873. Sheriff Jacob L. Gylam, a Texan, was called Jack by the Anglos and Jackicito by the Hispanics. David C. Warner was another Texan who had moved to the valley. They both liked their liquor. So did Tom and Ben Horrell and their buddy Zachariah Crumpton. Having had too much to drink, the group decided to "shoot up" the streets of Lincoln. They were raising quite a ruckus when Constable Juan Martín approached and asked them to surrender their guns. Gylam insulted his fellow law officer and told the group to ignore him. The hell-raisers then headed toward a brothel, shooting their revolvers into the air as they walked down the street. Martin rounded up a mob of fellow Mexicans that included Seferino Trujillo and Juan Patrón. When Martin and his men arrived at the brothel they knocked on two doors of adjoining rooms which were occupied by Tom Horrell and Dave Warner. One or the other shot and killed Martin. Warner was shot to death in the return of fire. When the gunfight started, Ben Horrell and Jack Gylam ran from the brothel. They were chased down the street and cornered by the mob. The Hispanics then riddled both men with much lead. In his report to the Adjutant General, Major John Mason, commandant at Fort Stanton, wrote that "the Texans were murdered in cold blood, one at least (Ben Horrell, just 20 years old) while on his knees badly wounded, had surrendered and begged for mercy, was inhumanly murdered by having been pierced by nine balls his body then taken and thrown across the creek near the town." None of the bodies were removed until the following day. Gylam's body was found with thirteen slugs in it. During the night someone had cut off one of Ben Horrell's fingers in order to steal his gold ring. Prior to daybreak, someone had carved a cross on the forehead of Juan Martín.

Three days later two Mexicans were found dead in a pasture at the Horrell Ranch. The following day, the 5th of December, newly appointed Sheriff Alexander H. "Ham" Mills led a large posse to the Horrell homestead and demanded they surrender. The Horrells refused. Shots were fired by both parties sporadically throughout the day. No one was injured. Ham Mills and his posse returned to Lincoln early that evening, without prisoners.

On the 20th of December, a Saturday night, the Horrells and their friends rode into Lincoln. They went straight to a house where a Mexican wedding dance was in progress. The Anglos poured a barrage of lead into the house before riding off into the darkness. They left behind four dead and three wounded. Killed were Isidro Patrón (Juan's father), Isidro Padilla, Mario Balazan and José Candelaria. Wounded were Balazan's nephew and two women, Apolonia Garcia and Pilar Candelaria.

On January 7, 1874, Governor Marsh Giddings posted rewards of $100 each for Zach Crumpton, Jerry Scott and three Horrell brothers (actually there were four). This act "officially" made them fugitives from the law. It also gave anybody the right to bring them in. Six days later L. G. Murphy, J. J. Dolan, William Brady and José Montaño organized a vigilance committee for the purpose of eliminating the Horrells once and for all.

Realizing that their time in New Mexico was limited, the Horrells sold nearly 1,100 head of cattle, a few horses and oxen for the sum of

$9,802.50. On the next day (January 20) Sherff Mills and a large posse of Hispanics surrounded the Horrell ranch. That night, under the cover of darkness, the Horrells slipped away and moved down river to the Casey ranch. One day later, Ben Turner (brother-in-law of the deceased Ben Horrell) and a boy named Edward "Little" Hart made their way to the house of a Hispanic in order to procure some corn. Ben Turner was ambushed and slain.

Realizing that the Horrells had abandoned their ranch, J. J. Dolan and a group of opportunists rode to the site. After pilfering the Horrell house they "confiscated" crops and other items which they hauled back to Lincoln.

Incensed by the course of events, the Horrells decided it was their turn to reciprocate. They sent word to Lincoln that they were heading to town for a "reckoning" with L. G. Murphy, J. J. Dolan, Steve Stanley, Ham Mills, Juan Patrón, Juan Gonzales, Bill Warnick and Joe Haskins. Most of the men in the Horrell clan departed for Lincoln on Friday, January 30th. They were armed to the teeth. At Picacho, C. W. King, Edward "Little" Hart and Tom Kennan detoured to the Haskins' homestead. When Joe opened the door, they shot him dead as his horrified Hispanic wife watched.

At some point on the road to Lincoln, the Texans decided to abandon their plan, possibly because they had foolhardily given their opponents advanced warning of their coming. They chose to raise a little more havoc and then head to Texas. The Horrells decided to raid the ranches of some of their enemies and steal their horses before departing from New Mexico.

With the wagons full of their women and children (escorted by Merritt Horrell and a few other men) safely out of the area on a southerly route, the rest of the men turned east along the Rio Hondo. They pillaged the ranches of Ham Mills and his half-brother Steve Stanley. They stole whatever horses they could gather and rode hard down river toward Missouri Plaza (Missouri Bottom). When they reached the settlement of Roswell, the Horrells raided the ranches of Van C. Smith and Aaron O. Wilburn driving off all of their horses. The band then turned south along the Pecos River.

Along the trail, the Horrells encountered the wagons of five Hispanic teamsters who were freighting corn to the South Spring River ranch of John Chisum. The Horrell bunch assassinated all five Mexicans Pablo Romero, Juan Silva, Severiano Apadaca, Severiano Aguilar and Reymundo Aguilar.

The next target of the Horrell gang was the ranch of Hugh Beckwith at Seven Rivers. Beckwith, like Ham Mills and Steve Stanley, was married to a Hispanic woman. A few miles north of the ranch, the group encountered Robert Beckwith (Hugh's oldest son) from whom they stole a horse, saddle and gun. Shortly thereafter, they ripped down a corral fence and drove off Hugh Beckwith's horses.

Meanwhile, Aaron Wilburn and Van C. Smith had rounded up a posse which began tracking the horse thieves to the south. Wilburn and Smith were both known to be excellent marksmen. Van C. Smith was a former sheriff of Yavapai County, Arizona, and later would become a deputy sheriff under John Behan at Tombstone, Arizona. They recruited additional riders at Seven Rivers. Eventually the Horrells' trail turned west toward El Paso. Realizing that the Horrells would probably sell the stolen stock in El Paso or Mexico, the posse hastened its pace.

At some point, the horse thieves joined up with Merritt Horrell and the wagons carrying the women and children. This slowed their movement toward El Paso. Smith, Wilburn and the posse spotted the Horrell clan at a place called Hueco Tanks, about 30 miles east of El Paso. Once they were within shooting distance, the posse rained lead on the Horrell band. Zach Crumpton was killed instantly. Three other members of the clan were wounded. Fearing for the safety of the women and children, the Horrells waved a white flag in order to negotiate with the posse. Smith and Wilburn agreed that if the Horrells would return their horses, their caravan could proceed without further harm. Smith and Wilburn cut out their horses, and then headed north. At this point, it seems as though the Horrell band turned back to the east in the direction of Fort Davis.

Further down the road, the Horrells encountered a tribe of Apaches. The clan drew their wagons together as a defensive precaution. The party of Indians remained at a distance and only observed. While this was happening one of the wounded men died (a fellow named Steele or Still). The Horrells buried him, and then built a fire over his grave so the Apaches wouldn't discover it. Eventually the Indians moved on without incident. After they did, the Horrells also left.

The clan headed back to Lampasas County. "The Horrell War" in New Mexico was over, but problems between Anglos and Hispanics would continue. Later (for the murders which occurred at the Mexican wedding dance), the Grand Jury would hand down indictments against Sam and Merritt Horrell, Jerry Scott, Zach Crumpton (who was deceased), Robert Honeycutt, James Wilson, Edward Hart, C. W. King, Thomas Bowen (Bill Bowen), Captain James Randlett, Robert Casey and others. An attempt was made to prosecute Randlett and Casey. Randlett obtained a change of venue to Socorro County, where his case was thrown out of court. Charges were eventually dropped against Casey, and warrants were never served on any of the others.

The Horrell party arrived in Lampasas County determined to

keep the peace. Almost immediately, however, there was an altercation with the sheriff and his posse. Merritt Horrell and Jerry Scott were wounded during the conflict about which the newspaper later reported that "no shots were fired by the Horrell party." Merritt Horrell and Bill Bowen agreed to stand trial for the death of Captain Tom Williams and the other members of the State Police. When the case was finally heard in October of 1876, both men were acquitted. The Horrells were making an effort to lead a peaceful life, for a change. Their passiveness would not last for long, however.

Although the feud between the Horrells and Higgins actually began in 1877, its roots go back four years earlier. The Higgins family first established a ranch in Lampasas County in 1857, about the same time the Horrells did. They were neighbors, and originally they were friends. Several incidents turned the friendship into a bloody feud. John Calhoun Pinckney Higgins, usually known as "Pink", was incensed in 1873 when the Horrells killed one of his in-laws, the aforementioned State Police Captain Tom Williams. While riding line one day, Pink Higgins heard a distant shot. He decided to ride out and investigate. He found Zeke Terrell butchering a cow with a Higgins brand. Pink Higgins unsheathed his rifle and killed Terrell on the spot. According to legend, Higgins stuffed Terrell's body inside the disemboweled cow, then notified authorities where they could find the occurrence of a miracle, a cow giving birth to a man. Zeke Terrell had been a Horrell employee. Ike Lantier was a former Quantrill raider who cowpoked for the Horrells. While watering his horse one day, he was startled by an approaching rider and drew his revolver. Pink Higgins, who had already drawn his weapon, fired a slug into Lantier's midsection and killed him instantly. On more than one occasion, Higgins accused the Horrells of tampering with his cattle. Tom Horrell was riding through the brush one day when he met Higgins, his henchman Bill Wren and brother-in-law Bob Mitchell. Quick tempered Pink Higgins cursed Horrell and threatened to kill him. According to the story told, the cool-headed Tom Horrell eased back in his saddle and said something like, "Well, three against one wouldn't be much credit to you." Higgins and his cohorts turned and rode off without further confrontation.

January 22, 1877, was a cold day. Merritt Horrell was standing in front of a fire in the back of Jerry Scott's saloon, and was unaware that Pink Higgins had entered the building. Higgins shot Horrell twice, and after he crumpled to the floor Higgins shot him two more times. Merritt Horrell was dead. He never had a chance to draw or return fire. On the following day a posse of Texas Rangers brought four of Higgins' men into Lampasas for questioning, but Pink Higgins could not be found.

While en route to the Lampasas courthouse on the morning of

March 26, 1877, Tom and Mart Horrell were ambushed about five miles outside of town by Higgins men. Tom was knocked from his saddle as a slug ripped into his hip. Mart received a superficial neck wound but was able to valiantly drive off the attackers. Mart helped Tom reach the Tinnins homestead, nearby, and then hastened into town to report the incident.

About a month later, Pink Higgins and Bob Mitchell decided that they had been dodging the law long enough and surrendered to authorities. Both were allowed to post bond and return home.

There was another bloody occurrence about the first of June. At daybreak one morning, two of Higgins' cowboys stepped out of a line shack where they had bunked for the night. As they did so, they were shot down by a barrage of rifle fire. One of the men was killed instantly, while the other would live three more days. It is believed that Tom and Mart Horrell and Bill Bowen were responsible for the incident.

Another confrontation took place at the intersection of Third Street and Live Oak Street in Lampasas on the morning of June 7, 1877. Frank Mitchell and his father, Mack, were loading flour at the store of Yates and Brown on Third Street at about 10:00 a.m. Several members of the Horrell bunch had congregated near the well at Public Square adjacent to Live Oak Street. The group included Tom, Mart and Sam Horrell, Jim "Buck" Waldrup and Bob McBee. John Dixon and Rufus Overstreet of the Horrell faction were nearby at the home of Dixon's mother. When Pink Higgins, Bob Mitchell, Bill Wren and Ben Terry rode south on Live Oak Street they were spotted by the men at Public Square. The Higgins men also saw the Horrells. Shooting started immediately as everybody scattered for shelter.

Bill Wren took a slug in one hip but managed to drag himself up a flight of stairs to a second-story window from where he had a better vantage point. Pink Higgins spurred his mount and rode away to recruit help. Frank Mitchell, who was Bob's younger brother, opened fire on the Horrells from the front door of Yates and Brown. One of his shots dropped Buck Waldrup (who would die the following day). Mart Horrell returned the fire and killed Frank Mitchell where he stood.

Sporadic shooting continued for over an hour. At approximately 11:30 a.m. Pink Higgins returned with reinforcements. The men of both factions fortified themselves and nothing much happened after that. Early in the afternoon, impartial citizens were able to talk both parties into a cease fire.

The following month, fourteen Higgins riders raided the Horrell ranch. The Higgins men took positions surrounding the ranch house and bunkhouse from where they poured rifle fire at the Horrells. The Horrell brothers and their men fought back with a vengeance. After a two-day siege, the Higgins' ammunition began to run low. They departed leaving two Horrell men with minor wounds.

On the 25th of July, Carson Graham departed from the Higgins ranch and headed toward Lampasas to purchase supplies. He was ambushed on the road. Beside his body the Horrell brand had been etched into the dirt.

Major John B. Jones, who was commander of the Texas Rangers' Frontier Battalion, rode into Lampasas County with a detachment of reinforcements for the already present Rangers. Jones was determined to end the feud between the Horrells and Higgins one way or another. He exercised the first part of his plan by arresting five members of the Horrell faction. They were kept under guard at the Ranger camp in order to protect them from the Higgins bunch. Jones then arrested Higgins, Mitchell and Wren and put them under heavy guard at a separate location. This method would allow Major Jones to negotiate with each party without them having to come face to face with each other. His plan was successful. Both parties signed letters of truce. The first letter was dated July 30, 1877, and was signed by the Horrell brothers:

Lampasas Texas
July 30th 1877

Messrs Pink Higgins Robert Mitchell and William Wren.
Gentlemen:

John Pinckney Higgins was a cattleman who earned a reputation as being a tough, unyielding individual. *Center for American History, University of Texas at Austin (W. P. Webb Papers).*

From this standpoint, looking back over the past with its terrible experiences both to ourselves and to you, and to the suffering which has been entailed upon both of our families and our friends by the quarrel in which we have been involved with its repeated fatal consequences, and looking to a termination of the same, and a peaceful, honorable and happy adjustment of our difficulties which shall leave both ourselves and you, all our self respect and sense of unimpaired honor, we have determined to take the initiatory in a move for reconciliation. Therefore we present this paper in which we hold ourselves in honor bound to lay down our arms and to end the strife in which we have been engaged against you and exert our utmost efforts to entirely eradicate all enmity from the minds of our friends who have taken sides with us in the feud hereinbefore alluded to.

And we promise furthermore to abstain from insulting or injuring you and your friends, to bury the bitter past forever, and join with you as good citizens in undoing the evil which has resulted from our quarrel, and to leave nothing undone which we can effect to bring about a complete consummation of the purpose to which we have herein committed ourselves. PROVIDED: -

That you shall on your part take upon yourselves a similar obligation as respects our friends and us, and shall address a paper to us with your signatures thereon, such a paper as this which we freely offer you. Hoping that this may bring about the happy result which it aims at we remain

Yours Respectfully,
Thos. L. Horrell
S. W. Horrell
C. M. Horrell

Witness
Jno B. Jones
Maj. Frontier Battalion

Major Jones delivered the Horrell letter to Higgins, Mitchell and Wren. They responded with their letter of August 2, 1877:

Lampasas Texas
Aug 2nd 1877

Messrs Mart. Tom and Sam Horrell
Gentlemen

Tom Horrell, a man of calm demeanor, and his wife, Mattie Ann, a proud but boastful woman. *Sarah Harrison Cobb.*

Your favor dated the 30th of July was handed to us by Maj. Jones. We have carefully noted its contents and approve most sincerely the spirit of the communication. It would be difficult for us to express in words the mental disturbance to ourselves which the said quarrel with its fatal consequences, alluded to in your letter occasioned. And now with passions cooled we look back with you sorrowfully to the past, and promise with you to commence at once and instantly the task of repairing the injuries resulting from the difficulty as far as our power extends to do. Certainly we will make every effort to restore good feeling with those who armed themselves in our quarrel, and on our part we lay down our weapons with the honest purpose to regard the feud which has existed between you and us as a by gone thing to be remembered only to bewail. Furthermore as you say we will abstain from offering insult or injury to you or yours and will seek to bring all of our friends to a complete conformity with the agreement herein expressed by us.

As we hope for future peace and happiness for ourselves and for those who look to us for guidance and protection and as we desire to take position as good law abiding citizens and preservers of peace and order we subscribe ourselves

Respectfully &c
J.P. Higgins
R.A. Mitchell
W.R. Wren

Witness
Jno B. Jones
Maj. Frontier Battalion

Both factions were ready for peace. Each was sick and tired of the death, destruction, fear and mental anguish associated with the feud. Rarely is a truce between feudists adhered to, but this one was.

Pink Higgins remained in Lampasas until the turn of the century when he moved his ranching operation to the vicinity of Spur, Texas. He was responsible for a couple of other killings (which had nothing to do with the Horrells) before he died of a heart attack at age 66.

Tom and Mart Horrell were arrested for the May 28, 1878, murder of storekeeper J. F. Vaughan, thirty miles west of Waco. The two brothers were locked up in the jailhouse at Meridian on the 8th of September to await trial. On the night of December 15th, a large mob of masked men rode to the jailhouse, whisked past the jailer and with a volley of gunfire assassinated Tom and Mart Horrell in their cells. Many people thought that the Horrells were innocent of Vaughan's murder, but the brothers never had a chance to prove it in court.

Sam was the only remaining Horrell brother. In 1880 he moved back to New Mexico where he raised his six children. Sam Horrell died in California on August 8, 1936.

Major John B. Jones successfully negotiated a truce between the hostile factions in the Horrell-Higgins Feud. Jones, who was commander of the Texas Rangers' Frontier Battalion, also helped establish peace in the Hoodoo War at Mason. *Texas State Library & Archives Commission.*

Pink Higgins and some of his men. Back row (Left to Right), Powell Woods, Unknown, Buck Allen and A.T. Mitchell. Front row, Felix Castello, Jess Standard, Bob Mitchell and Pink Higgins. *Center for American History, University of Texas at Austin (W.P. Webb Papers).*

Clay Allison recuperates after shooting himself in the foot. The wound occurred as the former Confederate soldier attempted to stampede U.S. Army mules near Cimarron, New Mexico in 1870. *Bill H.Hubbs, Barney Hubbs Colleection.*

Chapter Five
Bad, Bad Clay Allison

Trouble often followed Clay Allison, but he seemed to thrive on it. Though normally an easy-going individual, he was known to be quick tempered and impulsive on occasion. Because of these traits, and some questionable deeds, history has depicted Robert Clay Allison as rather violent. In one incident, after a mob lynched an accused murderer in Cimarron, New Mexico, Allison supposedly decapitated him and displayed his head on a pole in a local saloon. Following another vigilante-style lynching, Allison allegedly tied the rope end opposite the noose to his saddle horn and dragged the corpse over rocks. Two days later, Clay Allison gunned down a friend of the lynching victim.

Legend has it that during a cattle drive in Wyoming, Allison developed a severe toothache and visited a Cheyenne dentist. After the dentist accidently broke off one of his teeth, the enraged Allison forcibly extracted one of the dentist's front teeth.

On December 21, 1876, Clay Allison and his brother John had stopped in Las Animas, Colorado during a trip from their home in Texas.

The brothers were enjoying the revelry at the Olympic Dance Hall, but had entirely too much to drink. When they were approached by Charles Faber, a deputy sheriff, who asked them to check their guns, they simply ignored him. The Allisons loved the dance hall girls, and they enjoyed dancing, but sometimes carried matters to the extreme. The more they drank, the more belligerent they became. Before long they were trampling the feet of other couples on the dance floor.

Incensed by the course of events, Charles Faber lined up two deputies and returned to the Olympic Dance Hall. Faber had a double-barrel shotgun in hand. As Faber entered the building, John Allison was still on the dance floor. Clay was leaning against the bar with his back to the door. Someone hollered, "Look out!" John whirled to see what was happening. Faber thought John Allison was going for his gun and shot him in the chest and shoulder with a barrel of buckshot.

Clay drew and fired four quick shots at Faber. One pierced his chest, and the deputy sheriff fell dead on the floor. As Faber collapsed, the other barrel of his shotgun discharged striking John again. This time he was hit in the leg. Clay stepped to the entrance and fired several more shots at the other two deputies as they fled into the dark. Clay then dragged Faber's body over to his bleeding brother assuring him that vengeance was done. Clay Allison turned himself in, but was later released from custody. John eventually recovered from the buckshot wounds.

The incident was Clay Allison's last gunfight. A few years later, he married the sister of John's wife, and sired two daughters, the second whom he never saw. During his wife's second pregnancy, Clay Allison fractured his skull when he fell beneath a wagon near Pecos, Texas. He died almost immediately.

Sam Bass, who robbed banks, trains and stagecoaches, met his demise at Round Rock, Texas. *Denver Public Library, Western History Department.*

Chapter Six
Shootout at Round Rock

In late 1877 Samuel Bass rode out of Nebraska heading for Texas with money in his saddlebags, but he no longer had a gang. On the 18th of September, at Big Springs, Nebraska, the Sam Bass gang had recorded one of the most profitable train robberies in Old West history. The haul, which exceeded $60,000, was masterminded by one of the gang, Joel Collins. A week later Collins and gang members James Berry and Bill Heffridge were shot down, with the authorities retrieving $25,000. Bass returned to the Denton, Texas area where he had lived from 1870 to 1876.

Sam Bass began looking for new gang members. In Denton, he convinced old acquaintance Frank Jackson to ride with him. Jackson was a tinsmith who had gunned down a notorious horse thief a year earlier. In Dallas, early in 1878, he recruited Seaborn Barnes. Like Jackson, Seab Barnes was highly trusted by Bass, and both were loyal to him. Jim Murphy, who had a small ranch outside of Denton, decided to join the group. The freshly minted twenty-dollar gold pieces from the Big Springs heist that Bass was spreading around certainly didn't do anything to hurt his recruiting effort.

During the spring of 1878, the Sam Bass gang recorded four train robberies in the Dallas area. The robbers netted very little loot (just $150 from the Mesquite job). The holdups, however, precipitated a massive manhunt. On June 13, 1878, while camping at Salt Creek, in Wise County, the gang was surprised by a posse that was led by Texas Ranger Captain Junius "June" Peak. Gang member Arkansas Johnson was shot and killed. The others shot their way to safety and escaped on foot. Subsequently, they were able to steal some horses and headed to Denton County.

Jim Murphy began to feel the heat. He wanted out. He figured that if he simply left the gang, he would still be a wanted man, so he decided to cut a deal with the Texas Rangers. The Rangers agreed that robbery charges against Murphy would be dismissed if he would tip them off prior to the gang's next job. The opportunity came shortly thereafter at Round Rock, Texas.

On July 19, 1878, Sam Bass, Frank Jackson, Seab Barnes, and Jim Murphy rode into Round Rock. Murphy had already betrayed his companions, so the Texas Rangers, the local law enforcement officers, and the citizens of Round Rock were expecting trouble. Exactly when they were expecting it seems to be an unanswered question. There is speculation that the group arrived on the 19th only to case the bank, not to rob it. They may or may not have intended to rob the bank that day. Murphy dropped off at a store on the edge of town in order to avoid any trouble. Obviously, the plan was for him to reconnect with the others in town, if the robbery was scheduled to happen that day.

Regardless, Bass, Barnes, and Jackson tied up their horses on Lampasas Street adjacent to the alley that led to May Street. They walked about one and a half blocks to Koppel's Store, which was located on the corner of Main and Mays. In doing so, they passed Deputy Sheriff Moore who thought they might be carrying guns, which would have been a violation of the local ordinance. Moore, in turn, notified Deputy Sheriff A. W. Grimes and they also headed to Koppel's Store. Moore waited outside, and Grimes entered. Neither of the lawmen recognized the outlaws.

Grimes approached Bass and asked him if he was carrying any hardware. Bass whirled, drew, and fired. Grimes reeled backwards and dropped dead near the store entrance. As the group fled the store, they exchanged shots with Moore. The deputy sheriff took a bullet in the chest, but continued to shoot. One of his slugs hit Bass' right hand, near his ring finger. The gang ran for their horses.

Texas Ranger Dick Ware was at the barber shop, lying back in a chair with his face lathered awaiting a shave (one sign that they were not expecting trouble at the time). He charged out on to Main Street and gave pursuit, as did other lawmen. In the alley behind Highsmith's Livery Stable, near where the horses were tied, Seab Barnes was hit in the head by one of Ware's bullets and died instantly.

As Sam Bass neared his horse, he was hit again. The bullet entered near his spine, and exited beside his naval. He went down. His loyal cohort, Frank Jackson, while returning enough fire to hold their pursuers at bay, managed to help Bass up into his saddle.

The two rode north, and then west, to a densely wooded area about three miles from town. Bass had become too weak to continue. Jackson hastily bound his friend's wounds, and at the insistence of Bass, rode on alone.

The following morning, the badly bleeding Bass crawled from the woods to a railroad construction site nearby, where he received water from section hands. The posse picked him up there and returned him to Round Rock. He was thoroughly interrogated but refused to say anything about his gang. Bass did say that he thought Dick Ware had fired the shot that downed him, although records indicate that the shot was actually fired by Texas Ranger George Harrell. Sam Bass died the following day, July 21, 1878, on his twenty-seventh birthday. He, Seaborn Barnes, and A. W. Grimes were all buried in the Round Rock Cemetery, on the street later to be named Sam Bass Road, just west of the Chisholm Trail.

Jim Murphy got his deal. All charges against him for robbery were dismissed. Murphy returned to Denton. Fearing reprisals against himself or his family, they moved from his ranch to a house on East McKinney Street, which he felt would be safer. Murphy became very despondent, and a year later took his own life by swallowing atropine.

Evidently, Frank Jackson changed his identity and may have opted for a more peaceful life. The day he rode out of Round Rock, he did so into permanent anonymity.

Former confederate soldirer, Bob Lee, was a terror to the Union League following the Civil War. *Wild Horse Collection.*

Chapter Seven
The Lee-Peacock Feud

Most of the nation laid down their arms after General Robert E. Lee surrendered his Confederate forces at the courthouse in Appomattox, Virginia, in 1865. More than a year later, President Andrew Johnson declared that "there no longer existed any armed resistance of misguided citizens, or others, to the authority of the United States in any, or in all the States ... excepting only the State of Texas." The President's statement reflected the feeling in Washington that Texas was the only state that failed to totally comply with the "rules" of Reconstruction. One of the reasons was the Lee-Peacock feud, which in actuality was not a feud but simply a continuation of the Civil War. The conflict took place, for the most part, in the "Four Corners" region of northeast Texas, where Grayson, Collin, Fannin, and Hunt counties converge. In the midst of this area is a densely wooded 30 square mile (48 kilometers) thicket. It was a refuge for outlaws and deserters during the war.

Bob Lee lived in the northern part of the thicket. Although married, with three children, Lee volunteered for service in the Ninth Texas Cavalry of the Confederate States of America. Lee was not a slave owner. Most of his relatives and friends who served also fought for the CSA. The Maddox brothers, John, William and Francis, as well as several of the Boren clan had also joined the Ninth Texas Cavalry. A few men from the Four Corners area joined the Union forces, as well.

As the Civil War ended and it was time to head home, Bob Lee was hearing that trouble existed in his region of Texas. The Federal government had established the Union League, an organization created for the protection of former slaves and Union sympathizers. They set up their headquarters at Pilot Grove, just seven miles (11 kilometers) from Lee's home. Additionally, Union troops were in the area to help with the reconstruction effort. Residents of the Four Corners region considered the infringement and new laws as unwanted and unwelcome. When Bob Lee arrived home he was seen as the man who could minimize this new interference from the Feds.

Lewis Peacock was the head of the Union League. He resided just south of Pilot Grove. As he saw a mounting threat from Bob Lee and his followers, Peacock recruited men who were sympathetic to the cause of the Union League. Among those ready to assist Peacock were James Maddox, James Vaught, Hugh Hudson, John Baldock, some of the Boren clan, and a few of the Nance clan. Bob Lee could count on the help of Parson Martin Smith, the Dixon clan, as well as his own relatives of which there were many including his father and his brothers.

Bob Lee was awakened from his sick bed one night when a group of Union soldiers surrounded his house and informed him that he was under arrest for war crimes. They indicated that they had orders to take him to Sherman, Texas and demanded that he come with them. When they reached the Choctaw Creek bottoms, the soldiers took Lee's gold watch, a twenty dollar gold piece, and forced him to sign a $2,000 promissory note. Then they released him. Bob recognized the men who robbed him as Lewis Peacock, James Maddox, Israel Boren, Sam Bier, Hardy Dial, and Doc Wilson. Bob Lee wasn't about to agree to the note and headed to Bonham where he filed a suit in civil court against Peacock and his men. Lee won his case, but the battle had just begun.

In February of 1867, Bob Lee was in a grocery store at Pilot Grove where he came face to face with James Maddox. The two had words. When Lee turned to leave, Maddox fired a shot at the back of his head. The slug grazed his scalp and knocked him unconscious. He was carried to the home of Dr. William Pierce for treatment. A few days later while Lee was still at the Pierce residence, one of Peacock's men, Hugh Hudson, paid a visit. When Dr. Pierce opened his front door he was shot and killed by Hudson. Dr. W. C. Holmes, who was at the Pierce residence, was an eye-witness to the killing and would later travel to Saltillo, in Hopkins County, to identify Hudson (who had been shot) as Pierce's murderer. When Bob Lee swore to avenge the doctor's death, everyone in the Four Corners area armed themselves and locked their doors. The wrath of Bob Lee followed. During 1868 there were casualties on both sides. Among the dead were Billy Dixon, Lige Clark, Dow Nance, Elijah Clark, Dan Sanders, and John Baldock. Lewis Peacock and many others were wounded. Some of the deaths occurred as follows.

The Dixon clan supported Bob Lee. Elijah Clark was a Peacock man. During the spring of 1868, Clark called on Hester Anne Dixon to invite her in person to accompany him to a dance. While in the Dixon home he politely removed his pistol and placed it on a table. When Hester Anne refused the invitation, Clark left in such a huff that he forgot to pick up his weapon. In front of the house he ran into 16-year-old Billy Dixon. Elijah Clark was so disappointed that he grabbed Dixon's gun and shot him. Slightly wounded, Billy Dixon ran into the house, seized Clark's pistol, ran back outside and shot Elijah Clark who tumbled from his horse with a fatal wound.

A few weeks later, Billy Dixon and his cousin Charlie Dixon were transporting a load of cotton when their wagon broke down. They were about twenty miles (32 kilometers) from their respective homes. As they were fixing the buckboard, a group of Peacock's men rode up. One of the men shot and killed Billy at the roadside, and they proceeded to depart leaving Charlie unharmed.

After two of Peacocks men forced two Lee women to feed them a meal, they departed and quickly met their demise when they were blown out of their saddles just a short distance from the house. A meeting of the Lewis Peacock men was held at the Nance farm. When Bob Lee was tipped that the meeting was going to take place he gathered a group of his supporters. Once the Peacock men had assembled at Nance's horse lot, Bob Lee attacked. In the gunfight that followed three of Peacocks followers were slain. The dead men were Dow Nance, Dan Sanders, and John Baldock.

General J. J. Reynolds put a price on the head of Bob Lee. On August 27, 1868, he issued a proclamation offering a reward of $1,000 to anyone who could deliver Lee to the Post Commander at either Marshall or Austin. Three Union sympathizers from Kansas decided to take the general up on his proposition. They were found dead in the middle of the road not far from the Lee house.

Bob Lee was no longer spending nights at home. He knew that his life was in more danger than ever with the reward on his head. He had set up a hideout in the thicket and would only emerge when he was advised that it was safe to do so.

The Boren's were cousins of Bob Lee, but their family was split over their allegiance to the Union and to the Confederacy. They were correspondingly split in their support of the Peacock and Lee conflict.

Henry Boren fought for the Union during the war, but the other Borens cast their lot with the Confederacy. Bill rode with William Clarke Quantrill's raiders. Henry Boren was somehow able to find out where the trail was to Bob Lee's hideout in the thicket. He may have overheard a family member's conversation. One day in either May or June of 1869 (there are several conflicting dates) Bob Lee was ambushed and killed by Henry Boren and members of the Sixth Cavalry.

Before Bob Lee had been laid to rest, Bill Boren retaliated. Furious, he went to the home of Henry Boren and after some cross words shot and killed Henry. Bill claimed that Henry was armed and ordered him off his property. He added that he did not draw until Henry "pulled down on me." Bill Boren left the area to be with his friend, John Wesley Hardin. After several years had passed, Bill was enticed back to the Four Corners. He was subsequently killed by Henry Boren's son.

Dick Johnson and Joe Parker were Bob Lee men intent on killing Lewis Peacock. In early July of 1871 one of them (nobody knows which one) climbed a tree at dawn by Lewis Peacock's home. When Peacock came out to get wood for the wood stove he was shot and killed beside his house.

Things eventually settled down in the Four Corners area, and other places, and for the most part Texas abided by the laws and ideals of Reconstruction.

Daniel Riley "Dee" Harkey and his bride, Sophie New, on the occasion of their wedding in August of 1886. *Myrtle Fritschy.*

Chapter Eight
Dee Harkey: Guts and Grit

D. R. "Dee" Harkey became an officer of the law in 1882 at the age of sixteen. He wore a badge until 1911. Harkey was not quick on the draw, nor was he more than an adequate marksman, but he was long on guts. Also, he was either very lucky or he had a guardian angel for he was shot at many times. Dee Harkey had a great deal of compassion for other people. Few lawmen on the western frontier would ever give a man who had attempted to murder him a second chance. Dee could not shoot a man once he had "the drop" on him. Nevertheless, he was a highly effective lawman, even though he did things his own way.

Dee Harkey was born at Richland Springs, Texas, on March 27, 1866. One of thirteen children, he was orphaned when he was three years old. Dee was virtually raised by his oldest brother Joe (who was seventeen years old at the time of their parents' death). Joe was elected sheriff of San Saba County, Texas, in 1880. Two years later, Dee was sworn in as one of his deputies.

The first man that Dee Harkey ever arrested was one of the most hardened killers in the Old West, "Deacon" Jim Miller. In a San Saba saloon one night, Miller, Bill White and the three Renfro brothers had been raising a ruckus. When White struck a fellow who was currently on jury duty, the sheriff was beckoned. Within minutes, Joe and Dee Harkey burst through the lattice saloon door. Dee thrust his revolver in Miller's face. Deacon Jim raised his hands and said, "My God kid, don't kill me!" Dee took his gun. At the same time, Joe Harkey had disarmed White. The Renfro brothers were commanded to drop their gun belts, and they did. The Harkeys then marched the five down to the San Saba jailhouse and locked them up. All five were released the following day.

Joe Harkey had been advised by U.S. Marshal Gozlin, of San Antonio, to be on the alert for two bandits who had robbed a stagecoach near Mason. According to Gozlin, one of the men was tall and the other was shorter and heavyset. He further advised that there had been a $1,000 bill among the loot. Joe Harkey was informed that he would receive a $500 reward should he be able to arrest these robbers. It wasn't long before two men matching the bandits' description rode into San Saba. Joe recognized them as being former Indian fighters named Pitts and Yeager.

Dee was asked by Joe to shadow the suspects because he was young and they wouldn't pay much attention to him. Dee Harkey followed Pitts and Yeager to the bank where he saw them change a $1,000 bill. Before long, the robbers mounted up and rode out of San Saba. Joe and Dee trailed them at a distance. Pitts and Yeager rode east about 45 miles to the town of Lampasas. From there they turned to the southwest and headed to Llano. They were generally heading back toward the location of the stagecoach robbery. Joe Harkey decided to confront them in Llano. Pitts and Yeager had stopped at a blacksmith shop to have their horses shod. On the pretext of having their own horses shod, Joe and Dee were able to get close to the bandits, at which time the Harkeys drew in unison and arrested the fugitives. Joe Harkey received his $500 reward plus another $500 for delivering the bandits to Marshal Gozlin at the Lometa railroad depot. Joe had made a nice bonus on Pitts and Yeager, while his little brother gained valuable experience as a lawman.

Gozlin, Pitts and Yeager never reached San Antonio alive. When the Santa Fe train arrived into Austin, the wives of Pitts and Yeager and the mother of one of the wives were allowed to board the train and accompany the fugitives to San Antonio. Unknown to Gozlin they had smuggled weapons aboard. When the train was about seven miles south of Austin, Gozlin was shot in the back of the head. He died instantly. Gozlin's deputy and a conductor who quickly armed himself opened fire on Pitts and Yeager. During the exchange of fire the mother was shot through the stomach by the deputy. One of the fugitives was killed and the other wounded so badly that he would die shortly thereafter. Joe Harkey had warned Gozlin that Pitts and Yeager would kill him if they had a chance. Gozlin was careless, and Harkey was right.

Dee Harkey was shot at often during the many years he wore a badge, but he was only hit once, and it was by a girl. Harkey was quite fond of Mary Quinn who lived at Richland Springs. He escorted her to several dances and other events. When Joe Harkey instructed Dee to arrest Mary's father for stealing two mules, duty prevailed over emotion. As Dee attempted to make the arrest, Mary appeared with a cocked revolver. "Dee, that's my father and I'm going to protect him," she stated, then pulled the trigger. The bullet was deflected by a silver watch in Dee's vest pocket causing nothing more than a superficial wound. Dee Harkey never made the arrest. It was soon discovered that Quinn was an escaped convict wanted for murder. Shortly thereafter he killed the sheriff of Coleman County and was gunned down by several deputies.

On August 4, 1886, Dee Harkey married Sophie New, a young teenager who lived in Bee County, Texas. They were able to obtain a marriage license over the objections of Sophie's mother who tried to block the marriage because of her daughter's adolescence. Dee turned in his badge and rented a farm at Torro Creek (in Bee County) from a fellow named George Young. One day Young accused Harkey of abusing a steer he had sold him. It was the beginning of some bad blood between the two. Young attempted to badger Harkey into a fight, but the latter would have none of it. The landlord then turned some of his horses out in Harkey's cornfield where they destroyed part of his crop. George Young was plowing his garden of sweet potatoes when Harkey approached him to discuss the damage to his corn. Both men were carrying knives. Heated words quickly turned into a fight, and each man pulled his knife. Young, the larger of the two men, threw Harkey to the ground and cut him several times. Finally, while Young was on top of him, Harkey thrust his blade into his foe's back. Young leaped to his feet and ran toward his house while yelling at his wife to bring his shotgun. Once inside his house, George Young collapsed and died. Dee Harkey was arrested, charged with murder, and spent twenty-one days in jail before bond could be posted. When the case came to trial he was acquitted.

In 1890, Dee Harkey moved to Eddy, New Mexico (later to be renamed Carlsbad). He worked as a grocery clerk and then as a butcher. Before long, Harkey received an appointment as a deputy U.S. marshal. His instructions were to clean up Eddy County. Phoenix, just south of the community of Eddy, was a mecca of saloons, dance halls, gamblers and prostitutes. Furthermore, the condition existed because most of the county officials were saloon owners or pawns of those men who controlled the vice in Eddy County. The sheriff, Dave Kemp, was a partner in the largest gambling hall in Phoenix. His primary concern was to protect the interests of the saloon owners. Gambling was licensed in the territory and was a legitimate business, but the extensive rings of prostitution were not. Dee Harkey made this problem his number one priority.

The saloon owners built rows of little shacks (or cribs as they were commonly called) where their prostitutes could live and peddle their wares. The girls would work in the dance halls until about midnight, and then escort their partners to the cribs for further entertainment. Late one night, Harkey and two deputies raided several of the cribs. They hit the cribs one at a time, and did so quietly so no one would realize what was happening. Sixteen couples were arrested and whisked off to a train bound for the Socorro jailhouse. Nobody knew what had happened until the following day. Saloon owners were incensed. Threats against Harkey's life were commonplace. That night, Harkey and his deputies struck again. Sixteen more couples were hurried away to the train, and subsequently the jail at Socorro. The county officials were Republicans who previously had no opposition. Dee Harkey and other solid citizens organized the Democratic Party in Eddy County. A primary election was held in order to nominate a ticket to oppose the Republicans. On the day of the general election, Democrats swept the Republicans out of office. Gradually, the undesirable elements began to pull out of Phoenix and head for greener pastures.

One evening during the spring of 1895 a gunfight broke out in Phoenix, between a group of about fifteen Mexicans and an equal number of Anglos. The Mexicans were led by Tranquellano Estabo, who was handy with a gun. The Anglos, were from Eddy, and were led by Walter

Looking north on Canyon Street in Eddy, New Mexico, in 1893. Six years later the community was renamed Carlsbad. *Southwestern New Mexico Historical Society of Carlsbad.*

Paddleford. When words erupted into gunfire, Estabo's bunch dove to the ground behind the railroad tracks. The fellows from Eddy scrambled for cover behind several barrels which were filled with empty beer bottles. When Dee Harkey rode onto the scene, three Mexicans had been killed and one wounded, while one Anglo had also been slain.

As lead flew in both directions, Harkey approached and ordered both factions to cease fire. The Mexicans stopped firing, then so did the Anglos. Harkey walked between both groups, and then approached the Anglos. Paddleford stepped forward. He tore his shirt open and pointed to his bare chest, advising Harkey to shoot him there. He exclaimed, "My dad was a war horse and I was his papoose, and you are afraid to shoot me." Harkey simply snatched the Winchester from Paddleford's hand, and then marched the whole bunch off to jail.

Harkey would have further confrontations with both Paddleford and Estabo. Paddleford jumped bail and headed to Mexico. Harkey tracked Paddleford to Sonora, Mexico, where he arrested him again. Armed with a writ which assured them safe passage out of Mexico, Harkey and his prisoner returned to Eddy County. Once again, Paddleford was allowed to post bail. He jumped bail again and disappeared. No further effort was ever made to bring Walter Paddleford to trial. During the summer of 1895, Tranquellano Estabo killed a fellow gambler during a quarrel at Phoenix. When Dee Harkey attempted to arrest Estabo, the Mexican shot at him then rode out of town at breakneck speed. Harkey chased the fugitive on horseback for three miles before catching up with him. Estabo pleaded, "Don't kill me! Don't kill me!" Harkey escorted Estabo to the Eddy County jail and locked him up.

Before he escaped from the penitentiary in Texas, Jim Nite had been serving a life sentence for killing a cashier during a bank robbery. Nite fled from Texas to New Mexico where he formed a new outlaw gang. They were a ruthless bunch that robbed and killed as they moved about the territory. After the gang rustled some horses in Eddy County, Dee Harkey and three deputies set out to track them down. Whereas the outlaws had plenty of fresh horses and could simply swap saddles from one to another, the posse had to stop on the second day. They shod their horses using felt from a hat as a liner. It allowed the horses to continue. On the third day, Harkey encountered a goat herder who told him that five men had stolen all his food, guns and ammunition the night before. Dee knew he was on the right track. Two days later, the lawmen arrived at a ranch house that Nite had robbed of all the supplies he needed. The lawmen picked up fresh horses and continued their chase.

Harkey flagged down a Rock Island Railroad train in order to procure water for their horses. It was discovered that Nite had held up the train one day earlier. At this point, a fellow named Tom Tucker joined the posse. He was a former Hash Knife cowboy who participated in the Pleasant Valley War in Arizona. At daybreak the following morning, the lawmen stumbled onto the fugitives while they were still in camp. Harkey's men were able to scatter the outlaws' horses before an all out gun battle erupted.

Harkey was pinned on a knoll between his deputies (who were above and behind him) and the outlaws below. He knew he could not move from his position without being hit. So, he unmercifully rained lead on Nite and his men. With their horses gone and a hail of bullets dropping from above the outlaws quickly surrendered. The ordeal was over.

Jim Nite was returned to the penitentiary in Texas to finish serving his life sentence. His four confederates escaped from jail and headed in different directions. Will Morrow was captured in Montana. Dan Johnson was caught in Arizona. The two were returned to New Mexico where they were tried and convicted. The other fugitives made good their escape.

When Dee Harkey retired from service as a lawman he remained in Eddy County as a successful rancher.

Volney Gibson, a Jaybird, was one of the central figures in the political feud at Richmond. *Fort Bend Museum.*

Chapter Nine
The Jaybird-Woodpecker Conflict

Richmond, Texas, was the scene of a political rivalry that ultimately turned into a blood bath. In the late 1880s the population of Fort Bend County was nearly eighty percent Black. The reins of political power were controlled by the Woodpeckers, who consisted of carpetbaggers, local Republicans (who wouldn't admit to being Republicans), and a few prominent Blacks, all of which were controlled by the Black vote. Jaybirds, on the other hand, consisted of the majority of the Caucasian population—that which one would consider to be "Southern white." Jaybirds accused Woodpeckers of much graft, which included assessing taxes based on one's political views. Much hatred grew between the two factions. The division was political, racial and social.

How the two groups got their strange names is a matter of speculation. County administrators were sometimes called Peckerwoods, which probably evolved into Woodpeckers as the term Jaybirds became popular. Presumably, the upstart Jaybirds received their title from the Blacks because they were "uppity like a jaybird." On July 2, 1888, the

Jaybirds officially launched the Young Men's Democratic Club of Fort Bend County. The club was organized "to secure a wise, impartial, economical and unselfish administration of the affairs of our county"; and furthermore to terminate the rule by "the arbitrary and selfish minority that has so long disregarded the consent of the governed." They were fighting words. The battle lines had been set.

The leader of the Jaybirds was H. H. Frost, a merchant who operated the Brahma Bull and Red Hot Bar, a general store and saloon. He was aggressive, vivacious and had guts which helped earn him the nickname "Red Hot" Frost. Though a saloonkeeper, Frost had a little religion. Carry Nation (later to gain fame as a temperance advocate), who conducted a Sunday school class, once said of him, "One poor saloonkeeper named Frost came several times and always gave a dollar." The forces behind the Woodpeckers were James Wesson Parker, a member of the State Legislature, Sheriff Jim Garvey, and Jake Blakely, a former sheriff.

Justice of the Peace, J. H. Shamblin, an active Jaybird, was shot to death at his home on the 2nd of August. The murder was committed by William Caldwell, a Black who was facing trial in Shamblin's court for cotton theft. Caldwell was tried, found guilty, and was executed by hanging. Although Shamblin's murderer seemingly had no political roots, Jaybirds blamed Woodpeckers for the incident.

Several minor altercations intensified the brewing feud. On

Judge J. W. Parker was a driving force behind the Woodpeckers. *George Memorial Library.*

August 16, 1888, a barbecue was held in Pittsville at which several Jaybirds and Woodpeckers nearly came to blows. On the 30th of August a Black man named Jim Bearfield came into Richmond from an outlying settlement. He had been wounded in the neck and hand and his face was drawn with fear. While he was in his house, somebody shot at him through an open door. According to Bearfield, he was attacked because he knew the identity of a man who was involved in the whipping of two Blacks the previous week. Bearfield swore out a warrant against H. H. Frost. Frost retaliated by suing Bearfield for perjury. Neither case ever went to court.

H. H. Frost locked the doors of his Red Hot Bar on the evening of September 3rd and was walking home when the still night was rattled by two shotgun blasts. Buckshot struck Frost in his right arm and destroyed his hat. Two days later a large assemblage met at the courthouse at which time it was determined that seven undesirable Blacks should be run out of town. Among those Blacks was a county commissioner, two schoolteachers and the district clerk. Following a little verbal sparring and an ultimatum, the seven reluctantly agreed to leave town.

Prior to the election of 1888 another barbecue was held. Jaybirds, Woodpeckers and those without political affiliation attended. The gathering, which was held at Duke's Station, ended in a confrontation between Volney Gibson (a Jaybird) and Kyle Terry (the Woodpecker candidate for county assessor). During his speech to the mixture of partisans, Terry referred to Ned Gibson as a "paper-collared dude." Volney Gibson, who was probably the best marksman in Fort Bend County, took offense to Terry's remark, and retorted, "Ned isn't here, but I'll represent him!" Kyle Terry accepted the challenge and leaped from the platform with his revolver already drawn. Members of the crowd grabbed him and trouble was averted—at least for the time being.

When the votes were counted, the Woodpeckers retained control of the county offices. Once again, it was the Black vote that decided the election. When invitations were mailed out for the Woodpeckers' victory celebration many were sent to Jaybirds. The Jaybirds remailed their invitations to Black prostitutes, an insult which infuriated the Woodpeckers. A few days later, Kyle Terry approached Volney Gibson regarding the invitations which had been remailed by Jaybirds. If Gibson had been armed, gunplay certainly would have occurred. The incident was followed by other encounters. Kyle Terry's distaste for the Gibsons was like a fuse waiting for fire.

On the afternoon of January 21, 1889 at Wharton, as lawyer Ned Gibson walked toward the courthouse, he was dropped in his tracks by a blast from the shotgun of Kyle Terry. Ned Gibson died immediately. Although there was no immediate retaliation, the slaying was a declaration of war

Much of the fighting occurred in front of the Fort Bend County Courthouse where several Woodpeckers had taken refuge. *Fort Bend Museum.*

to the Jaybirds.

A detachment of eight Texas Rangers, led by Sergeant Ira Aten, was dispatched to Richmond to prevent further bloodshed. Several months of relative calm passed, but the town was like a powder keg just waiting for a spark to set it off. As fate would have it, four of the Rangers had been called out of town, and another lay ill in camp when all hell broke loose on August 16, 1889.

It was early evening as Judge J. W. Parker and his nephew, W. T. Wade, rode west on a Richmond street. Volney Gibson and his brother Guilf were riding east on the same street. As they approached each other Parker and the Gibsons drew and began shooting. Parker whirled his horse around and raced toward the courthouse. Ignoring Wade, the Gibsons gave chase. One of the slugs found its mark, hitting Parker in the back. He was able to dismount and take refuge inside the courthouse. The shots were heard by Woodpeckers, Jaybirds and others. Within moments there was a crowd in the streets. Sheriff Jim Garvey and two deputies were nearby and rushed to the aid of Parker. H. H. Frost emerged from his Brahma Bull and Red Hot Bar with a group of Jaybirds which included DeRugely Peareson, Yandell and Keane Ferris, Jeff Bryant, Charles Parnell and Will Andrus. When he heard shots, Sergeant Ira Aten and two Rangers dashed to the scene. Aten tried to intercede but was ordered away by Sheriff Garvey. Several Woodpeckers rushed to the side of Garvey who had taken up a position behind the iron fence which separated the courthouse from the street. As the Rangers looked on helplessly, bullets flew in both directions. The leaders of each faction were the primary targets. Shots dropped both Garvey and Frost. Garvey pulled himself up, fired a couple more rounds, then fell over dead. As the former sheriff, Jake Blakely, came into sight, the wounded Frost gunned him down. Blakely died instantly. Judge Parker, whose wound had been wrapped, emerged from the door of the courthouse. As he did, a bullet from the upstairs window of the McFarlane residence hit him in the groin. Once again, Parker struggled to safety inside the courthouse. With the leaders down, the shooting finally stopped.

The McFarlane house where three youths, Earle McFarlane, Dolph Peareson and Sid Peareson, manned the upstairs windows. From this vantage point Judge J. W. Parker was shot as he emerged from the courthouse. *Fort Bend Museum.*

As previously mentioned, Garvey and Blakely were dead. Frost would die two days later. A Black girl, Robbie Smith, had been killed by a stray bullet as the Gibsons encountered Parker (Parker and Wade were later charged in the murder). Parker would recover from his wounds. Volney Gibson, W. T. Wade, Will Andrus, Frank Schmidt and H. S. Mason also received minor injuries which would eventually mend. Following a request for the militia, Governor Ross dispatched the Houston Light Guard to Richmond as a peacekeeping force.

There were several arrests and a few lawsuits during the aftermath of the Jaybird-Woodpecker hostilities in Fort Bend County. Ira Aten became the new sheriff. Many of the Woodpeckers moved out of the area. The Jaybirds seized control of the county government, a position they would hold for many years.

The trial of Kyle Terry for the murder of Ned Gibson was set for January 21, 1890, at the courthouse in Galveston. Before ascending the steps to the criminal courtroom, Terry came face to face with Volney Gibson. Gibson drew a pistol and shot Kyle Terry in the heart. Before he could be brought to trial for killing Terry, Volney Gibson died of tuberculosis on April 9, 1891.

Richmond, Texas, in 1892. *George Memorial Library.*

The community of Mason, as it looked in 1876. *Mason Historical Commission.*

Chapter Ten
The Hoodoo War

Fort Mason, Texas, was officially established on July 6, 1851. It was one of many forts located on the Texas frontier to protect settlers from Indians. The site, on the bank of Comanche Creek about eight miles north of the Llano River was set just above the community of Mason which was named county seat when Mason County was established in 1858. Many German immigrants settled in the area. For the most part, they established ranches and raised cattle. They constructed solid stone buildings for permanence and protection.

Results of the 1860 census showed that Mason County had a population of 630. When votes were cast on February 23, 1861, on the issue of secession, only two votes were recorded "for" while seventy-five were cast "against." Few German settlers were slave owners, and they wanted no part of the slavery issue. When Texas seceded from the Union to join the Confederacy, the Germans in Mason County were generally despised by the non-German element as traitors. As anti-German prejudice grew, two factions emerged—the German and the Anglo. The lines between the factions were quite fuzzy. Though most Germans seemed sympathetic to the Union cause, many fought for the Confederacy. The Civil War years marked a period of many Indian atrocities in Mason County. White settlers, both German and Anglo, banded together to protect themselves from the Indians. Nevertheless, animosity between Anglos and Germans was real.

While most of the ranchers and cowboys from Mason County were off fighting for the Confederate Army, their cattle would drift away by the thousands. Some people made a living out of rounding up strays and selling them at market. Later, when laws were passed requiring all cattle brands to be recorded, some of these same people became cattle rustlers. After the ranchers and cowboys returned from the battlefields, there became some assemblage of control over their herds. When the massive cattle drives began, they crossed the vast open range of Mason County on their way to the cow towns of Kansas. Local ranchers faced the new difficulty of preventing their cattle from joining the herds that passed through. Ranchers faced another problem during cold winters. Severe weather would often cause cattle to drift south. As they crossed the open ranges other cattle would join them. Sometimes these herds numbered in the thousands.

By 1872 Mason County ranchers had begun to string miles and miles of barbed wire fencing in an effort to control their herds. These wire fences heightened the discord which already existed between ethnic groups. Furthermore, it pitted cattleman against cattleman. In some cases, the barbed wire prevented access to water. When wire crossed the path of a herd being driven to market, cowboys would normally cut the wire rather than change direction. An increasing number of cattle rustlers in Mason County added to the amount of fence cutting, as well as the number of flared tempers.

Mason County had been divided, neighbor against neighbor, cattleman against rustler, German against Anglo, and even brother against brother. The stage was set for much violence in what was to be called the Mason County War, more popularly known as the Hoodoo War.

In late 1875, a local rancher, Tim Williamson, was arrested for rustling by Deputy Sheriff John Worley. While Worley, a lawman of German descent, was escorting Williamson to jail they encountered a large and angry mob. Williamson never had a chance to prove his innocence, nor did he ever reach the jailhouse. Without making any attempt to break up the mob, Worley stood by and watched as they shot Williamson down in cold blood. The execution raised the ire of Williamson's friends.

One such friend was Scott Cooley, who owed a lot to the Williamson family, possibly even his life. While in Kansas, at the terminus of a cattle drive, Tim Williamson met and befriended Cooley. Williamson offered Cooley employment as a hired hand in Mason County. Cooley accepted, and then accompanied the cowhands on their trip back to Texas. While working for Williamson, Cooley became seriously ill with typhoid fever. Mrs. Williamson spent many long days nursing Cooley until his health was restored. He was indebted to the Williamson family. After leaving Williamson's employment, he joined the Texas Rangers where he was a member of Captain R. C. (Rufe)

Perry's Company D. Cooley had left the Rangers and was working near Menardville when he received word of Williamson's assassination. Scott Cooley packed up some supplies and rode toward Mason County heavily armed.

Cooley had several friends in the little town of Mason. He spent a few days asking questions and gathering information. Having learned what he wanted, he set out for Deputy Sheriff John Worley's place. As Cooley approached the house he spotted two men working on a windless at the well. Cooley, who did not know what Worley looked like, asked one man his name. His reply was, "Worley." It was the only identification needed. Cooley drew and shot the deputy sheriff to death. Worley's helper plunged into the well. Cooley dismounted and scalped his victim. Uncertain who the next victim might be, fear ran high through the German faction. Other friends of Tim Williamson decided to ride with Scott Cooley. He was joined by Mose and John Beard, George Gladden and John Ringgold.

Another incident occurred in Mason where mob justice prevailed. Sheriff John Clark had locked up five rustlers who had been caught while driving a herd of cattle that belonged to others. With battering rams, the mob shattered the jailhouse door, and then dragged the rustlers into the street. They marched their prisoners about a half mile down the Fredericksburg road. By the time Sheriff Clark and a few others reached the scene, the mob had scattered. Clark found a fellow named Wiggins lying on the ground dead. He had been shot through the head. Three of the rustlers were hanging from a tree limb. Two brothers named Baccus were dead. Clark cut down the third man, Turley, who was still alive. During the commotion of the lynching, the fifth rustler, Johnson, had managed to jump a fence and disappear across a plowed field.

Dan Hoerster was a prominent member of the community and a leader of the German faction. He had become a target of Scott Cooley. One day as Hoerster, Peter Jordan and a fellow named Pluenneke were riding past the Southern Hotel in Mason, a shotgun blast knocked Hoerster out of his saddle. He would die of buckshot wounds from the gun of John Beard. As Beard, Cooley and George Gladden galloped out of town, a slug from the rifle of Peter Jordan shattered Gladden's hand and the rifle he was holding.

Several days later, Sheriff Clark was inside Keller's store on the Llano River about twelve miles south of Mason. Keller and Clark spotted two men approaching the store. They were recognized as Mose Beard and George Gladden, two of Cooley's men. After Beard and Gladden dismounted, Clark and Keller opened fire from the front door. Gladden and Beard returned the fire, but with nowhere to hide they were hit by many slugs. Somehow they managed to mount one horse and ride away. Clark, Keller and another man trailed the wounded duo. Beard and Gladden were bleeding badly and had to stop. Clark and the others found them shortly. Minutes later Mose Beard died. Gladden had nine slugs in his body, and was expected to die. He was taken by wagon to his home in Loyal Valley. Gladden would eventually recover.

After regaining his strength, George Gladden shot and killed Peter Border, known as a gunman for the German faction. Gladden was captured and sentenced to 99 years imprisonment. Before long, however, he would be pardoned and released.

John Ringgold was arrested and jailed in Burnet County. Evidently, there was no evidence linking him to any of the crimes, and he was released.

Major John B. Jones was commander of the Frontier Battalion, Texas Rangers, which was comprised of six companies that patrolled approximately four hundred miles of border. When the governor asked the Texas Rangers to intervene and shut down the trouble in Mason County, Major Jones was selected for the task. With a detachment of forty men (ten from Company D, and thirty from Company A), Jones rode to Mason. Jones launched a massive manhunt for Scott Cooley. After two weeks of searching, and no trace of Cooley, Jones realized that his men were not taking the search seriously. Most of the detachment was in sympathy with Cooley, who had ridden with Company D when he was

Formerly a member of the Texas Rangers, Scott Cooley, was a major participant in the Hoodoo War. *Mason Historical Commission.*

a Texas Ranger. Reluctantly, Jones called his men together to make them an offer. He advised them that any man who was in sympathy with Scott Cooley and who did not wish to pursue him could step forward and receive an honorable discharge. About fifteen men took Jones up on his offer.

John Clark, having had his fill of violence, resigned from the office of sheriff and left Mason County. John Beard also fled the area. Some say he went to Arizona. Through the mere presence of Major Jones and the Texas Rangers, the Hoodoo War came to an end. Scott Cooley disappeared. Some say he became ill and died the following year (1876) in Blanco. Others say he lived to a ripe old age in New Mexico.

Deadly killer "Deacon" Jim Miller was lynched at Ada, Oklahoma, in 1909. *Western History Collections, University of Oklahoma Library.*

Chapter Eleven
Bulletproof Killer and the Pecos Grudge

James B. Miller (commonly called Jim, Deacon, or Killer Miller) was a killer for hire, whose number of victims probably equaled those of any gunfighter on the western frontier. He was an assassin who usually ambushed his prey. Miller was rarely involved in a "fair" fight.

G. A. (Bud) Frazer was a Texas Ranger and a deputy sheriff of Pecos County before his election as sheriff of Reeves County, Texas, in 1890. Miller became one of the Frazer's deputies.

An incident occurred in Reeves County which probably precipitated the bad blood between Frazer and Miller. Miller shot and killed a Mexican prisoner, then advised Frazer that he had tried to resist arrest. When the truth became known, that the prisoner had been killed because he knew that Miller had stolen a pair of mules, Bud Frazer fired him.

Miller ran against Frazer for the office of sheriff in the election of 1892, but was resoundly defeated. Shortly thereafter, Miller was appointed Pecos city marshal. The bitterness between the two grew.

Miller decided that he had had enough of Frazer and decided to assassinate him. In May 1893, Miller and two cohorts planned a scheme to stage a mock shootout at the railroad depot upon Frazer's return from a business trip. The third member of the party would shoot Frazer with a "stray" bullet from a hiding place. Somehow Frazer got wind of the plan and arrived in Pecos with two Texas Rangers.

Frazer knew that Miller would try again. But, he finally got tired of being apprehensive. On the morning of April 12, 1894, while Miller carried on a conversation in front of a Pecos hotel, Frazer approached and opened fire. His first shot hit Miller in the chest. The second struck him in his right arm as he began to draw. Miller reached around with his left hand, drew and returned the fire, but did so ineffectively as he was not left-handed. One bullet hit the ground and another struck Joe Kraus, an innocent bystander. Meanwhile, Frazer continued to fire. Three more shots hit Miller in the chest while Frazer's final shot struck him in the stomach and Miller collapsed. Thinking Miller was dead, Frazer walked off. Miller was seriously wounded, but would recover. He was wearing a steel breast plate which stopped the slugs fired at his chest.

During the election of 1894, Frazer lost his bid for re-election, and then left town. He returned to Pecos on the 26th of December to settle his affairs. In front of Zimmer's Blacksmith Shop he spied Miller and drew. The gunfight that unfolded was almost a replay of the previous one. Miller took Frazer's first slug in the right arm, once again rendering the arm useless. He drew and began to shoot with his left hand. A second bullet ripped Miller's left leg. When the third and fourth shots hit him in the chest and he continued to stand, Frazer turned and ran. Evidently nobody had told him about the steel breast plate.

The stage was set for the third and final encounter between Miller and Frazer. The event, which occurred on September 13, 1896, was no contest. Bud Frazer was seated at a poker table in a saloon at Toyah, about twenty miles southwest of Pecos. Jim Miller stepped to the saloon door, leveled his shotgun, and killed Frazer with a load of buckshot to the head.

Deacon Jim Miller killed many over the ensuing years. It came to an end in 1909, when Miller was lynched with three others in an Ada, Oklahoma livery stable for the killing of local rancher Gus Bobbitt. Miller's last request was that his hat be placed upon his head.

Creed Taylor, shown above, and his sons Hays and Phillip (nicknamed Doboy) were prominent figures during the early years of the Sutton-Taylor Feud. *The Center for American History, University of Texas at Austin.*

Chapter Twelve
The Sutton-Taylor Feud

Following the surrender by General Robert E. Lee at Appomatox in 1865, thousands of dejected Confederate soldiers turned toward home. The beaten and downtrodden warriors hadn't received a paycheck in ages, their clothes were torn and ragged and their feelings ran high with animosity. Their ill will was not only targeted at the Yankees who defeated them, but often at fellow Southerners who remained at home making money in cattle, cotton and slaves while they impoverished themselves in the army of the Confederacy. When the South failed to fit the mold expected by Congress, they passed the Reconstruction Acts which heightened the agony that already existed in the South. Animosity continued to run high as Federal troops supported carpetbaggers, scalawags and former slaves who were thrown into various governmental positions. In Texas, there was very little social order even after the arrival of the occupation forces. Many former Rebel soldiers set out to re-establish what they felt was rightfully theirs, and some did so with minimal regard for the law and governmental authority.

Prior to the days of barbed wire, Texas cattle roamed free on unfenced open range. Cattle often drifted far from their home range, especially during that time when most of the cowboys were away fighting the war between the states. When a maverick (an unbranded calf) had been weaned, it was fair game for the cowboy who "found" it and applied his brand. The stealing of cattle became big business. Sometimes when cattle were found with brands that were unfamiliar in the area, the finder might register the brand locally and claim ownership of the cattle. Another practice was to register the brand in a different locale, then drive the herd to market at that location. Many rustlers altered brands to make them look completely different. Counterbranding was another means of identification used by the cattle thief. He would cancel the original brand by burning an "x" or diagonal bar through it, and would then apply his own brand as if he had legally purchased the animal. Many former soldiers found rustling to be an easy means to obtain wealth.

Rustlers ran rampant while federal, state and county law enforcement officials did little to stop them. Either they were incapable of doing so or it was a matter out of their "domain." Ranchers decided to take matters into their own hands. Committees of vigilance, called Regulators, appeared in several counties. These forces were often large, heavily armed and occasionally even had the blessing of the governor. Rustlers were not the only target of the Regulators. Their "duties" often included dispensing of known outlaws and others who had been branded as "undesirables." At the top of their "most wanted" list, in the area southeast of San Antonio, were the sons of Creed Taylor, Hays and Phillip. Phillip was known by his nickname "Doboy." The boys were tough, cool-headed and excellent marksmen.

The Taylor boys were continuously in trouble. One incident occurred in an Indianola saloon while Hays Taylor was standing at the bar. A group of black soldiers entered and stepped up to the bar. When Hays advised them that he was not in the habit of drinking with blacks, shooting broke out. Hays shot two of the soldiers then quickly fled the scene. Shortly thereafter, a few miles outside of Indianola, Hays Taylor encountered another squad of black soldiers. They were convinced that he was fleeing from something and wanted him to return to Indianola with them. Taylor refused. A sergeant fired a shot which wounded Hays in one arm. Hays quickly responded by shooting the sergeant who toppled dead from his mule. As the other soldiers scattered, Taylor fled. On another occasion, in November of 1867, Hays Taylor was reading a newspaper while sitting propped against a hitching post, just outside a Mason saloon. Doboy Taylor and several friends were inside partying. As a group of Fort Mason soldiers approached the saloon, one of the privates badgered Hays. The private popped up the brim of Hays' hat and asked him what a damned reb could find of interest in a newspaper. Hays straightened his hat and continued to read. Spurred on by Hays' passive attitude, the private grabbed the hat again and yanked it down over Taylor's eyes. Hays drew and fired as he leaped to his feet. His slug dropped the private where he stood. He was dead. As this happened, one of the Taylor bunch, possibly Ran Spencer, was emerging from the saloon. He also fired, killing a Union sergeant. Major Thompson, the commandant at Fort Mason, arrived at that moment with his pistol in hand. He ordered the boys to surrender. With his usual quickness, Hays Taylor shot Major Thompson between the eyes. One version of this story indicates that the sergeant was actually killed after the slaying of Major Thompson. Regardless, the Taylor bunch rode out of Mason leaving three dead Union soldiers behind.

Buck Taylor (whose given name was William Riley Taylor, Jr.) was a first cousin of Hays and Doboy. His father, William, was one of Creed's brothers. Buck was attending a dance one evening at the home of Joe Tumlinson, his uncle. A squad of Union soldiers approached the house unnoticed. As they stepped through the doorway, a black sergeant pointed his finger at Buck Taylor. Buck drew his revolver and fired, killing the sergeant instantly. Amid the confusion which followed, Buck Taylor escaped to safety through a back door. He was another hunted man who rode with Hays, Doboy and the others.

A substantial reward was offered for the capture of the Taylors. Two fellows named Littleton and Stannard set out to find the Taylors and claim the reward. Littleton had exclaimed, "I will do it or die." Shortly thereafter, Littleton and Stannard were found dead on a road east of San Antonio.

The leaders of two groups of Regulators were summoned to Austin in early June of 1869 to meet with the governor. Jack Helm was a rather unscrupulous individual who led a group of Regulators which had been organized by his boss, A. H. "Shanghai" Pierce, a cattle baron who operated in the area southwest of Victoria. The other leader summoned by the governor was Captain C. S. Bell, a former Union spy and army scout. Helm, Bell and their Regulators, backed by state and Union officials, unleashed a reign of terror across DeWitt County and points south. In Galveston, the *News* reported on September 23, 1869, that "...during the months of July and August they killed 21 persons and turned 10 others over to the civil authorities."

The Choates (who lived in San Patricio County) were friends of the Taylor clan, and were suspected by Jack Helm of harboring some of the Taylor gang. On August 3, 1869, the Regulators attacked the Choate homestead killing John Choate and Crockett Choate and wounding two others. One of the wounded men, F. O. Skidmore, survived after receiving seventeen wounds, possibly the result of a shotgun blast.

After creating plenty of havoc in San Patricio County, Jack Helm met C. S. Bell near Yorktown in DeWitt County where the two planned their attack on the Creed Taylor ranch which was located on the Ecleto in Karnes County. Helm and Bell were aware that Hays and Doboy Taylor were in the vicinity but that the fugitives had been camping away from the ranch each night in order to avoid capture. The Regulators put their plan into action. C. S. Bell and his men rode directly to the Taylor place while Helm and the others remained in Yorktown as a diversion. Helm's bunch would follow, in order to arrive at Creed Taylor's house sometime after dawn. It was late Saturday night when Bell surprised Creed Taylor and the women. After placing Creed and the women under guard inside their home, the Regulators hid their horses and then waited in anticipation that Hays and Doboy would arrive in the morning. They were correct in their assumption. At daybreak on the 23rd of August, Doboy and Henry Westfall approached the house on horseback. Hays and their other companions were a short distance behind them. When she heard the horses, Doboy's wife let out a bloodcurdling scream in order to warn them. Doboy and Henry spurred their mounts and raced away amid a hail of gunfire. Hays spotted Creed who had emerged from the house. Believing that his father was in danger, Hays charged the whole posse of Regulators with his gun blazing. One of his slugs hit a posse member in the head wounding him seriously before a barrage of lead took Hay's life. As Jack Helm and the other Regulators rode toward the Taylor place that Sunday morning, they received word that C. S. Bell and his group had departed in pursuit of Doboy Taylor. Doboy and his comrades were able to elude C. S. Bell.

Two weeks later, Doboy and his friends were surprised by another posse at Pennington, Texas. After one of their men was shot to death, Doboy and a fellow named Cook surrendered to the posse. Along the trail to Crockett, Taylor and Cook made a break for freedom, and successfully escaped under the cover of darkness.

Meanwhile, Creed Taylor had been taken into custody by a couple of C. S. Bell's men. Creed was escorted to Helena where he was jailed. After spending approximately one month behind bars, Taylor was released under a bond of $10,000.

The activities of Helm and Bell created such a furor in southern Texas that Jack Helm felt compelled to publicly justify his actions. He did so in a report which was published on September 23, 1869, in the *Victoria Advocate*:

> "TO THE PEOPLE OF TEXAS: As there has been so much said by the people of the State regarding my operations, and as many know not of what they speak—attributing to me

motives that are false—I take this occasion of enlightening the law-abiding citizens as to what I have done, and why I did it. About the first of June I was duly summoned by the military authorities, through Captain C.S. Bell, special officer, to assist in arresting desperadoes in Texas known as the 'Taylor party.' We found this party near the rancho of Mr. Creed Taylor and attempted to arrest them. We succeeded in wounding one, Spencer by name, the other effecting an escape. I now proceeded in company with Bell to the City of Austin, where I received emphatic orders to arrest the party. On my return home I found that about forty had collected, in open defiance of the law, determined to resist the legal authorities of the State. I immediately proceeded to summon good citizens to assist me in the capture. The sheriff of DeWitt County accompanied me, myself being deputy sheriff. Both our lives had been threatened by these desperadoes, as well as the lives of all those co-operating with me for their arrest. Mr. Jacobs, the sheriff of Goliad County, had just been killed by members of this same party. Finding that I was ready and determined in action, they divided, separating in squads of from five to fifteen. I proceeded in pursuit of the strongest of these bands, commanded by Jim Bell, a noted desperado of DeWitt County. I succeeded in capturing him and more, who were afterward killed in attempting to escape from the authorities.

"About this time the Peaces—the murderers of Jacobs—were arrested, but subsequently effected an escape. One Stappwas killed in attempting to do so. The Peaces proceeded to the rancho of John Choate, in San Patricio County, stating to Choate that they were pursued by a 'vigilance committee', and that they came to him for protection. John Choate now went to the rancho of Joe Tumlinson in DeWitt County, fifty or seventy-five miles from his home, and informed Captain Tumlinson that he had left the Peace boys at his house, and that he had loaned them one hundred and fifty dollars with which to effect an escape to Galveston. Choate insisted that Tumlinson should join him; said he had a band well fortified at his house, fully able to whip Jack Helm anywhere. Choate also averred that Helm was a d—d rascal, and had joined the Yankees for popularity, and that he could not raise over thirty men, and they only Dutch and Yankees. Tumlinson told Choate that he knew Helm to be a good man, acting under proper authority, and that he intended to co-operate with him; that he knew the Peaces to be murderers and thieves; that he had hunted them, and would do so again.

Becoming convinced that Joe Tumlinson was not his man, Choate proceeded to the rancho of Creed Taylor, about fifty miles (80 kilometers) distant, where he remained about three days, when he came to the neighborhood of Yorktown, in company with four or five desperadoes, Hays Taylor among the number. Choate now sent word to Tumlinson if he did not join him he would be killed, and that the Yankees had offered twelve hundred dollars reward for him, for the supposed killing of Stapp. Tumlinson replied that if he had done anything wrong he was willing to surrender to the proper authorities of his country, but would have nothing to do with Choate or any of his gang. Choate replied that Tumlinson must risk the consequences of his folly. Choate now went by the house of Jim Bell, and took the clothing and other effects of the Peace boys to his house in San Patricio County. Here he met the Peaces, Fulcrod, the Broolans, Doughtys, Gormans, Perrys, and about forty-two others, all known desperadoes, and many having indictments against them for thieving. Choate informed them that Jack Helm would be upon them, and that they must prepare for a fight. The house was fortified and put in condition for a regular siege, having loop-holes cut on all sides, and secret passages connecting them room to room. They had one keg of powder, five hundred shot-gun cartridges, two hundred Spencer rifle cartridges, prerarations for receiving five hundred gallons of water, provisions, and all that was necessary for conducting a siege fifty days by fifty men. I had with me one hundred and twenty-five of the best citizens of the country. Arriving at Choate's a little after day, expecting to have to fight one hundred desperadoes, I immediately proceeded to carry the house by storm. I had one man killed and two wounded in the attack. Crockett and John Choate were killed, and two others wounded. Choate perfidiously attempted to shoot me after he had surrendered, and was killed by myself in defense of my life. I now made all the necessary preparation for interring the dead, which was done. And right here let me nail to the counter those lies that allege that my men disturbed any of Mrs. Choate's property or the property of anyone else. They did no such thing. I encamped in the neighborhood of San Patricio, and conferred with Captain Smith at Corpus Christi. I now proceeded to Yorktown, and sent a report to Helena. I was met at Yorktown by C.S. Bell, and disbanded my force until I could find out the whereabouts of the Taylors. Spent three days in this matter; collected my men, about twenty-five, and proceeded to the forks of the San

Antonio and Guadalupe rivers, where I succeeded in arresting the Hogans, who were members of the same party. I now sent the prisoners to Helena under charge of Tom Flemming and six others. I then proceeded in pursuit of the Taylors. At Yorktown I met Bell, and detailed fifteen men to accompany him, stating to the boys that Captain Bell was a good and true man, and would lead them. I remained in camp with the remainder of my men, to attract attention while Bell could operate. The next morning I took up the line of march for Creed Taylor's, followed by one hundred men. I proceeded by a circuitous route up the Sandies, arresting all persons that I suspicioned, and cutting off all means of escape. I arrived within seven miles of the house, when I received intelligence of the fight with the Taylors. I here disbanded my men, after complimenting them for their orderly conduct, gentlemanly bearing, and devotion to the lawsof the country. Taking ten men, I proceeded to Helena, where I met Majors Crosland and Callahan, Lieutenant Thompson, and other gentlemen, who approved of all I had done.

"I and my men are ready at all times to act with the legal authorities of my country in the enforcement of law and suppression of crime. I am a citizen of DeWitt County—deputy sheriff—and am opposed to mob law; but I am ready to give my assistance to the authorities, either civil or military, to arrest thieves and desperadoes who defy the laws, either in Texas or any other part of the United States, regardless of all threats, knowing that the law-abiding citizen is my friend, and the desperado my enemy, which is the only guaranty that I desire to know that I am right. *Jack Helm.*"

In sharp contrast to the report of Jack Helm, F. O. Skidmore wrote (several years later) a very different version of the raid in San Patricio County (which is duplicated here without notation of spelling, punctuation, capitalization or other grammatical errors):

"I was at Choate's ranche, in San Patricio County, Texas, on the 3d of August, 1869. Being an intimate friend of the family, I always stopped there when passing, and convenient to do so, and that was the case on this occasion. Not anticipating any trouble, I went, the 2d of August, 1869, to his house to remain all night; when I arrived at the house Mr. Choate was not at home, but soon arrived, and told me to put out my horse and stay with him all night.

"We conversed much that night about the reports in circulation regarding the high-handed measures of Jack Helm's party. Choate informed me that he had sent off the 'Peace boys,' so that he would not get into trouble on their account; he also said that he would fight any mob, but that any authorized officer—Federal or State—could come and take him and all his effects. I can't say that I saw anything more than usual going on at the house. There were only two men on the place except negroes; there were myself and two small boys, one my brother, aged fourteen years, the other about the same age.

"Helm's party charged the house about daybreak. I awoke at the first sound, and heard them yelling 'Charge!' Immediately several of their number rushed into the house.

"Crockett Choate shot a man named Kykendall. They retired to shelter in out-houses, behind trees and the yard fence. Mrs. Choate then appeared on the piazza, and held a parley with Helm. She informed him that Mr. Choate would surrender if he, Helm, had the authority to make the arrest.

"Helm replied that he was authorized by the highest authority in the State of Texas—orders from military headquarters. Mrs. Choate then informed him that there were three boys in the house who had stopped for the night, and that they were innocent, and for God's sake not to kill them. Helm replied, 'Tell the boys to come out, and they shall not be molested.' "When I heard that, I went out on the piazza, and spoke to those who confronted me, and I told them that I would surrender, and without a word of warning they commenced firing on me.

"I was shot seventeen times. When I returned to consciousness I was out in the yard near a tree. I crawled to it and sat up against it, and while in this position I was shot at several times; and as I sat there, I saw John Choate receive his first wound. As stated before, Helm said he had authority for his arrest; Choate came out in obedience to this demand, his wife accompanying him, and a little in advance. He raised both his hands above his head, and said, 'I surrender myself and house to the United States authority.' Choate, with the assistance of his wife, retreated to his room. The first wound was in the knee. I saw him no more alive. I was informed that they killed him outright immediately afterwards.

"When Crockett heard Mr. Choate surrender, he broke from the house with his six-shooter in his hand. He ran right past me, all the crowd following him. I then crawled away, and made my escape to a Mexican ranche about half a mile distant from Choate's house.

"About ten o'clock they pursued me there, and carried me back to the Choate house.

"When I arrived there Crockett and the old man were both laid out, dead. I begged them to take me to Mr. Terry's, but they would not. Said they wanted to watch the place. They conducted themselves in an extremely rough and boisterous manner while at the house, appropriating whatever they desired, as if they had killed a robber chieftain and had a right to appropriate his effects. They left me nothing, not even my clothing and pocket change. They stole my saddle, six-shooter, and other things of less note. I cannot say what was taken from the house. Helm talked in a braggadocio style to Dr. Downs, my attending physician.

"The house fronts south; old man Choate was in the east room; Crockett, myself, and the two boys were in the west end. Crockett fired a great many times. John Choate did not fire a gun that I could see or hear. His sole aim appeared to be to save his life. He appealed to Captain Tumlinson, as a Mason, to save him. Captain Tumlinson claimed that he was not present just then, but I saw him soon afterwards.

"Helm's party went to San Patricio from Choate's, but parties were continually lurking about the neighborhood for a week, which kept the neighborhood in a state of anxious suspense. I was six weeks confined to bed, unable to help myself at all. But, thank God, I have lived to see such things done away with.

"Crockett Choate was killed about three hundred yards from the house."

On the 23rd of November in 1869, a group of Regulators arrived at the ranch of W. B. Morris in McMullen County. There they captured Morris' son-in-law, Martin Taylor, whom they had been chasing. McMullen County had no court or jailhouse, so the Regulators set out with Taylor and Morris bound for the jail at Oakville in Live Oak County. The bullet-riddled bodies of Taylor and Morris were discovered the following day along that route.

When Edmund J. Davis took oath as governor of Texas in 1870, the here-to-fore quasi-legal Regulators no longer had the blessing of the state's highest office. It wasn't necessarily because Governor Davis was more ethical than former Governor Reynolds. He simply wanted control of the state's military forces. With the loosely-knit Texas Rangers (temporarily) disbanded, Davis was instrumental in organizing the Texas State Police, which would become a highly unpopular organization. Jack Helm was one of four captains named to the new force. Many of the officers recruited by Helm were former members of his old group of Regulators. Two of these were Jim Cox and Joe Tumlinson who were very anti-Taylor. Another of Helm's key comrades was Bill Sutton. Sutton was hated by the Taylors. Buck Taylor and a fellow named Dick Chisholm had been shot to death outside a Clinton saloon on Christmas eve in 1868 following a disagreement with Bill Sutton. Buck Taylor had just returned from driving a herd of horses to market in east Texas. Evidently, part of the herd consisted of some Sutton horses which Taylor included in the drive (for a fee). When he later found out that Sutton's horses had been stolen, Buck confronted Bill and called him a horse thief. Sutton and his compadres were never brought to trial.

Several months prior to the incident at Clinton, Bill Sutton shot and killed a suspected horse thief named Charley Taylor. The shooting occurred in Bastrop on the 25th of March. Charley Taylor may or may not have been kin to the Taylors of the area. If he was, the relationship was distant.

The DeWitt County Taylors indicated that they were not related to Charley Taylor, and possibly did so because he was a suspected horse thief. Two years earlier an incident occurred that may indicate otherwise, however. Charley Taylor shot a fellow named Polk whose wounded body was taken to the house of a Regulator, Captain John Littleton. He is the same Littleton that later set out to get Hays and Doboy Taylor stating, "I will do it or die." As previously mentioned, he and his comrade Stannard turned up dead.

Pitkin Taylor (brother of Creed) married Susan Cochran Day in the first marriage recorded in DeWitt County history. The couple had three children—a child who died at birth, Jim and Amanda. Additionally, Susan had three children from her prior marriage to Robert Day—John, Will and Betty. Amanda Taylor and Betty Day married brothers, Henry and William Kelly respectfully. They all lived in close proximity south of Cuero. Among their neighbors were Wiley and Eugene Kelly, brothers of Henry and William, as well as Susan's sons John and Will Day.

In mid-August of 1870 the Kelly brothers and their families traveled to the community of Sweet Home in Lavaca County to attend the performance of a circus. Apparently unhappy with the show, the Kellys proceeded to shoot out the lights. It was all the excuse Jack

Helm and Bill Sutton needed to continue their war against the Taylor clan. Early on the 26th of August, Bill Sutton, Doc White (who had been with Sutton when Charley Taylor was killed), John Meadows and Deputy Simmons (from Hallettsville in Lavaca County) rode to the homes of Henry and William Kelly and arrested the two brothers. With the Kellys, the lawmen set out on the road to Hallettsville. Amanda Taylor took a buggy and picked up her mother-in-law Delilah Kelly, with the intent of riding with the group to Lavaca County. In an obvious effort to lose the women, Sutton and his bunch took a "shortcut" through the brush where a wagon would be incapable of following.

In a later statement sworn before a Justice of the Peace, Amanda Taylor told how she saw her husband and brother-in-law killed in cold blood. She indicated that she had climbed from her buggy and ascended a rise overlooking the trail through the brush which the group had taken. She stated that the posse had stopped forty or fifty yards away and that John Meadows was no longer with them. William Kelly had dismounted and was attempting to light his pipe when Bill Sutton shot him. Instantly, Doc White shot Amanda's husband, Henry, and he toppled from his horse. The court later upheld the plea of the lawmen that they had shot the prisoners while in the act of attempting to escape. There was a huge public outcry following the Kelly murders. State Senator Bolivar Pridgen of Prices Creek in DeWitt County was extremely vocal about the killings. He condemned Jack Helm and the

Governor Edmund J. Davis organized the highly unpopular Texas State Police. *Texas State Library & Archives Commission (Photograph of a painting by William Henry Huddle).*

State Police for their methods. Newspapers across the state attacked the actions of Governor Davis. He felt the heat, which eventually resulted in the dismissal of Jack Helm from the State Police. This ouster had little effect on the citizens of DeWitt County, however, as Jack Helm still held the office of sheriff.

Doboy Taylor had "disappeared" for a while. He resurfaced in Kerrville in late 1871. With Jack Helm removed from the State Police force and C. S. Bell having moved out of the vicinity, Doboy could breathe easier. He applied for a position as agent for a cattle buying firm. When the firm hired Sim Holstein for the position, Doboy became incensed. From the gate outside Holstein's hotel, Doboy called the new agent out. The conversation over the gate became bitter. According to the *San Antonio Express*, on December 13, 1871:

> "Suddenly Taylor drew his pistol and fired at Holstein but overshot him—Holstein sprang over the gate, and before Taylor could shoot again, wrested his pistol from him and felled him to the ground with it. Taylor regained his feet, but was immediately shot down a second and third time. Then Taylor ran toward his house, calling on his friends for assistance. Another shot from Holstein brought him to the ground. His friends were prevented from doing anything by the determined attitude of Holstein. Taylor . . . survived six hours and died at

Pitkin Taylor and his wife Susan. At Pitkin's funeral their son Jim vowed to wash his "... hands in old Bill Sutton's blood". *Elizabeth Kelly Brautigam.*

11 o'clock the same night. He was sensible to the last, and spent his last hours imprecating and cursing the man he had attempted to murder."

Sim Holstein, unarmed when he approached the gate, was obviously a very tough individual.

One night (possibly September of 1872) Pitkin Taylor heard the bell of one of his oxen out in the cornfield. In his nightshirt he stepped outside to see if one of the oxen had wandered into his corn. As he did so, several shots rang out and Pitkin Taylor slumped to the ground. Pitkin, who was badly wounded, was moved to Lavaca County for safety. He lived for about six months, then died in March of 1873. According to the Taylor-Day-Kelly version of the story, Bill Sutton and four henchmen removed the bell from one of the oxen, slipped into the cornfield, and then rattled the bell with the certainty that Taylor would step outside.

Alfred Hays Day's account of Pitkin Taylor's funeral is as follows:

"It was a grim and tragic scene. The burial plot was near the river on a shaded knoll. Around the open grave the relatives of the murdered man were assembled. Among the mourners were young Jim Taylor, son of the deceased, and five other youthful kin of the slain man. In hideous contrast to this grief-stricken group, across the river while the funeral services were being conducted Bill Sutton assembled his cut throat [sic] gang in bold mockery. With raw drink and coarse jest and wild firing of guns they celebrated the death of Pitkin Taylor while he was being lowered into the grave.

"Hearing this hilarity, Jim's mother, who had borne up well under her grief, broke down and wept. If there had ever been a doubt in young Jim's mind what he should do about the slaying of his father, it was cleared up then. If ever a man was provoked into taking the law into his own hands Jim Taylor was justly provoked; if ever a man had reason to see that Justice [sic] was meted out, Jim Taylor was inspired by that reason.

"Putting his arm protectingly about his mother, he vowed to her: 'Do not weep mother [sic]. I will wash my hands in old Bill Sutton's blood!' The five other youthful relatives likewise pledged themselves to the same cause."

Bill Sutton was sitting in Bank's Saloon and Billiard Parlor at Cuero one Friday night when someone attempted to take his life. Two shots were fired into the building from the outside. One of the slugs penetrated Sutton's arm and side, wounding the lawman. On another occasion, Sutton and a few comrades were riding toward Clinton when they were ambushed. One of the men was wounded in the leg, and three of their horses were slain. No one knows who participated in either attack. We do know, however, that Bill Sutton was number one on the Taylor hit list.

John Wesley Hardin was one of the most dangerous gunfighters on the western frontier. In fact, he was probably involved in more gunfights than any other individual. In his autobiography, Hardin claims to have disposed of 44 men, but then he was known to be a braggart. About 25 percent of those deaths are verifiable through county records and documents. Many deaths, however, went unrecorded in those days. By the year 1871, eighteen-year-old Wes Hardin had already gained quite a reputation. As Hardin was being transported by the State Police from Marshall to Waco to stand trial (for a murder he had not committed), he killed a guard named Jim Smolly and escaped. Wes Hardin fled to Gonzales County to seek refuge at the ranch of his cousins, the Clements, south of the town of Smiley. He worked as a cowpoke and attempted to maintain a low profile. But Wes couldn't stay out of trouble. During the following year he was involved in several shootings, was wounded twice and was also captured. Wes' cousin, Emmanuel "Mannen" Clements, broke Hardin out of the Gonzales jail (in October of 1872) by slipping a file to Wes which he used to cut the window bars. Clements then returned and pulled Hardin through the opening with his lariat.

In April of 1873 at Cuero, Wes Hardin became involved in an argument with J. B. Morgan, a deputy of Jack Helm. There is a possibility that Morgan may have attempted to arrest Hardin while he was having a drink in a local saloon. Wes walked out of the saloon with Morgan in pursuit. As Morgan drew his revolver, Hardin whirled and shot the deputy in the head. Shortly after this incident, the Taylor faction gained some valuable recruits—Wes Hardin; Mannen Clements; his brothers Gibson, Jim and Joe; and Gibson's brother-in-law George Tennelle.

Shortly thereafter, Jack Helm led a large posse to Gonzales County, and the Clement's ranch, in search of Wes Hardin. The men were away rounding up strays, but Sheriff Helm succeeded in frightening Jane Bowen Hardin, Wes' new wife, and the Clements women. Incensed by the posse's visit, Wes Hardin, Mannen Clements and George Tennelle met with Jim, John and Scrap Taylor. They decided it was time to wage all-out war on Sutton, Helm, Cox, Tumlinson and the others. They wasted no time in taking the offensive.

On the 16th of June in 1873, Bill Sutton set out for Clinton to testify in the Bank's Saloon and Billiard Parlor shooting at Cuero on the 1st of April. Sutton was still recovering from his wounds, so he rode in a buggy. He was accompanied by Doc White, John Meadows, Horace French and Ad Patterson who were on horseback. Midway between Sutton's home and Clinton the group was ambushed. Meadows took a slug in one leg and French's horse was slain. There was no further damage. Feeling the heat, William and Laura Sutton moved to Victoria to get further away from the fighting.

One day in June of 1873, Jim Cox, Joe Tumlinson, H. Ragland and Jake Cresman were returning from the courthouse at Helena in Karnes County, where Cox was under indictment and had to answer certain charges. Tumlinson, who was his neighbor, Cresman and Ragland apparently went along for the ride. When the party reached the San Antonio River Tumlinson and Ragland opted for a different crossing than Cox and Cresman. It probably saved their lives. Jim Taylor, Scrap Taylor, Alf Day and Bud Dowlearn (whose mother was formerly a Taylor by marriage) were hidden awaiting the approach of the others. Suddenly a volley of gunfire erupted. The lifeless bodies of Jim Cox and Jake Cresman toppled from their horses. It is said that there were 19 buckshot wounds in Cox's body. Tumlinson and Ragland were far enough from the shooting that they were able to flee.

During the last week of July in 1873, Wes Hardin and Jim Taylor were at a blacksmith shop in Albuquerque, Texas where Hardin was having his horse shod. Jack Helm and a few friends spotted Jim Taylor and made a beeline to the blacksmith shop. Hearing the negative tone of the approaching voices, Hardin grabbed his shotgun and fired at Sheriff Helms. The blast scored a direct hit. Jim Taylor put several slugs in Helms' head to assure that he was dead. With Hardin's shotgun aimed directly at them, Helms' cohorts refused to participate in the action.

The Taylors received word that there was a large gathering of men at Joe Tumlinson's place. Realizing that the Sutton faction might be amassing for an attack, the Taylors decided to surprise them first. The Taylors, including Wes Hardin, crept toward the Tumlinson residence at approximately 2 a.m. They intended to get close to the porch where many men were sleeping, then open fire. Tumlinson's dogs detected the Taylors, however, and began barking loudly awakening the Sutton men who quickly took cover. Sporadic fire occurred throughout the siege which began early Tuesday morning and lasted until the sheriff and a large contingency of citizens talked the feuding parties into a truce sometime after daybreak on Wednesday. It was agreed that the principal members of each faction should accompany the sheriff to Clinton where a formal truce could be drawn up and signed. Both parties agreed, and the other participants were allowed to disperse and head toward their respective homes. The following account of this event occurred in the

Gonzales Enquirer and was reprinted in the *Houston Telegraph*:

"It is with no little gratification that we record a cessation of hostilities between the above name beligerents. It appears from the facts as related to us by a responsible party, that on Monday night last Wesley Hardin, accompanied with some 35 or 40 men, well armed, marched to the residence of Joe Tumlinson, in DeWitt County, surrounded his house and held him in seige for two nights and one day. In the meantime Joe Tumlinson and party, numbering 15 men, and strongly fortified, managed to dispatch a courier to Clinton for the sheriff to hasten to his assistance. After summoning about 50 men the sheriff started for the 'seat of war', where he arrived on Wednesday morning and found Hardin's men formed in line of battle. A brief conference with the parties revealed the unexpected but agreeable intelligence that a compromise had been effected between Hardin and Tumlinson; in other words, a treaty of peace had been agreed upon, and the two parties were ready to proceed to Clinton, a distance of 16 miles, and sign documents to that effect. The line of march was at once taken up. Hardin's men leading the column, the Sheriff's posse following, and Tumlinson's party bringing up the rear. Arriving at Clinton, Hardin halted on one side of the town, and Tumlinson on the other, while the sheriff's men marched directly into the town. After signing the documents and having the same recorded in the Clerk's Office, both parties quietly dispersed to the intense gratification of the law-abiding and peace-loving citizens."

In the Old West, it was rare when feudists adhered to the terms of a truce. This one lasted about four months before guns were blazing again. In late December, Wiley Pridgen (brother of ex-senator Bolivar Pridgen) was gunned down by unknown assassins near the entrance to Jim Pridgen's store in Thomaston. Several accounts have been given as to who the murderers might be, but nobody knew for certain. The Taylor faction, however, was sure that Bill Sutton was involved. The Taylors cornered Bill Sutton and some of his friends at the courthouse in Clinton. Realizing that their community might quickly become a battleground, Judge Henry Clay Pleasants and several of the town's women approached the Taylors and prevailed upon them to carry their feud elsewhere. They didn't want Clinton's citizens endangered or the town shot up. The Taylors agreed to take their fight elsewhere and hit the road to Cuero. Sutton and his men followed. Sutton sent a request for help to Joe Tumlinson, and then holed up at the Gulf Hotel in Cuero.

Tumlinson arrived with reinforcements and yet another siege wound up in a stalemate. Once again, both parties agreed to sign a truce—and they did. Although the newspapers voiced optimism, nobody really expected the feudists to adhere to this armistice either—and they didn't.

During the next few weeks three more men died, and another was wounded. One of the slain men was Bolivar Pridgen's ex-slave, Abraham Pickens (who had continued to work for Pridgen). Supposedly, Pickens was killed because he would not divulge Bolivar's whereabouts. Abraham's clothes were filled with rocks and his body was thrown into the river.

Word filtered through Bolivar Pridgen to Jim Taylor that Bill Sutton and his wife Laura were preparing to leave Texas via a ship departing from the port at Indianola. Joe Hardin (Wes' brother) and his cousin Alec Barrickman, both of whom were from Comanche, were visiting in DeWitt County. Wes Hardin persuaded Joe and Alec to snoop around (as they would not be recognized) to see what information they might obtain. They discovered that Bill and Laura Sutton were scheduled to depart on March 11, bound for the port at New Orleans. Jim and Bill Taylor followed the others to Indianola. Bill was a grandson of William Riley Taylor (brother of Jim's dad, Pitkin) and was therefore Jim's second cousin. Shortly after noon on the 11th of March in 1874, Bill Sutton, his friend Gabriel Slaughter and Bill's pregnant wife Laura were standing on the ship's deck waiting for the crew to cast off. Jim and Bill Taylor quickly approached. Jim Taylor shot Bill Sutton in the head and heart. Bill Taylor also fired and his slug hit Gabriel Slaughter in the head. Sutton and Slaughter were both dead as they fell at the feet of a distraught Laura Sutton. Before the Taylors fled, Jim seized Bill Sutton's ivory-handled revolver. Following this incident Laura Sutton offered a personal reward of $1,000 for the arrest of Jim Taylor (who already had a $500 bounty on his head).

The Taylors escaped to the house of Bolivar Pridgen in Thomaston, where the news was received with great joy. Pridgen had his cook prepare a lavish meal to celebrate the occasion. Jim Taylor helped Wes Hardin prepare a herd for its drive north. They decided to spend a few days in Comanche, then reunite with the drovers at some point on the trail. Bill Taylor decided to lie low in Texas. He didn't stay hidden enough, however, and was arrested by Reuben Brown, the city marshal of Cuero. Bill Taylor was transported to the jail at Galveston to await trial.

While in Comanche, Wes Hardin wagered on some horse races and won heavily. It was a nice present for his twenty-first birthday. His mood turned sour, however, when he learned that Charles Webb, deputy sheriff of nearby Brown County, was in Comanche with the intention of killing Hardin and collecting the $1,800 reward on his head. Wes was at Jack Wright's Saloon when Webb found him. Hardin offered to buy Webb a drink at the bar. As Charles Webb stepped toward the bar, he drew his revolver and fired. Alertly, Hardin jumped to one side as he drew his own pistol. Webb's bullet grazed Hardin who fired. His slug ripped through the deputy's head. Although he was already dead, as he fell, Bud Dixon (Wes' cousin) and Jim Taylor also shot him. They immediately fled the scene. A large and irate mob could not find Hardin and Taylor but were successful in capturing Bud Dixon. They also rounded up Joe Hardin and Tom Dixon (neither of whom were directly involved in the killing of Sheriff Webb). The three were locked up in the Comanche jail. Several days later an angry mob dragged the trio from the jailhouse and lynched them. Joe Hardin's cousin Alec Barrickman and Ham Anderson (two of Wes' stock hands) decided to hide at the house of Bill Stone. Barrickman and Anderson were discovered by a posse and shot to death. Another posse rode to Mason County where Hardin's drovers were holding his cattle. Three or four of the cowboys escaped. Doc Brosius (Hardin's trail boss), Scrap Taylor, Kute Tuggle and Jim White were taken into custody and escorted to DeWitt County. During the night of June 20, 1874, a mob broke the prisoners out of jail. Brosius was somehow rescued by a fellow Mason during all the commotion. The others were hanged from a tree near the Clinton cemetery.

    The hunt for Taylor men continued. A posse cornered George Tennelle at the residence of John Runnel in Gonzales County. When Tennelle refused to surrender, he was shot to death by the posse.

    The reward for John Wesley Hardin had been raised to $4,000. He felt the heat and knew it was time to leave Texas. He sent word to Jane who met him in New Orleans, and the couple then relocated to Pollard, Escambia County, Alabama where they stayed with friends (the Whitings) and assumed the aliases of Mr. and Mrs. J. H. Swain.

    By this time, Richard Coke had become governor, the State Police had been dissolved and the Texas Rangers rode once again. Citizens of DeWitt County pleaded with Governor Coke to maintain a detachment of Texas Rangers in the area as a peacekeeping force. He agreed to do so. In late July, Captain Leander H. McNelly led a force of forty Rangers into DeWitt County. McNelly was a tough individual who had an advanced case of tuberculosis (called consumption in those days), and he knew he was dying. It was probably the reason that he had no fear. McNelly's force maintained a highly visible profile and things began to settle down in the area.

    Bolivar Pridgen was successful in obtaining indictments against Joe Tumlinson and 26 other men for the murder of his employee,

Bill and Laura Sutton. Following the death of Bill Sutton, his wife, Laura, offered a reward for the capture of Jim Taylor. *The Center for American History, University of Texas at Austin.*

Prior to two devastating hurricanes, the port at Indianola once rivaled Galveston. This is where Bill Sutton was shot to death by Jim Taylor. *Calhoun County Museum.*

Abraham Pickens. Joe Tumlinson died of natural causes before he could be tried. It was probably for that reason that the case against the others never came to trial.

After two postponements, Bill Taylor's trial was scheduled for September of 1875. He was transported from Galveston to the jail at Indianola a few days before his case was to be heard. During the interim, a severe hurricane struck Indianola. As the Gulf surge raised the water

Scrap Taylor, an active participant in the feud, would often run with Alf Day and Jim Taylor. *Elizabeth Kelly Brautigam.*

level in Matagorda Bay, the Indianola jailhouse began to fill with water. Concerned that the prisoners (Taylor, two rustlers and a rapist) might drown, District Attorney Bill Crain released them, and the five men made their way to the second floor of the courthouse which was adjacent to the jail. That day, and the next, Bill Taylor and another prisoner named Blackburn joined in the rescue effort. Many people were saved due to the heroism of Taylor and Blackburn. After two days, the savage winds finally subsided. The death toll was large. Sheriff Fred Busch arrived on horseback (the 17th of September) and entered the courthouse to talk with the nearly 100 survivors who had found shelter there. During an unsuspecting moment, Blackburn snatched Busch's revolver from its holster. While holding the sheriff at gunpoint, Blackburn appropriated the lawman's horse. Blackburn and Bill Taylor mounted the animal and raced out of town.

Two months later to the day, City Marshal Reuben Brown was dealing Monte in the Exchange Saloon at Cuero when a few men walked in and shot him to death. Two black men at Brown's table were wounded as well. Although no charges were ever filed, it is believed that the responsible party consisted of Jim Taylor, Bill Taylor, Joe Bennett and possibly two others. The murder was obviously a retaliation for Brown's arrest of Bill Taylor following the killing of Bill Sutton. A few weeks later Bill Taylor and Joe Bennett were ambushed by unknown assailants near the town of Clinton. Bennett received a superficial wound before the pair escaped to safety.

On December 27, 1875, Jim Taylor and a large party of armed men rode into Clinton. Their purpose was uncertain, but Sheriff Weisiger was convinced that they planned to burn down the courthouse. Weisiger recruited the help of several citizens who were determined to defend the courthouse. Two members of the Taylor bunch were Tom King and his adopted brother Ed Davis. Their father, Martin King, owned the blacksmith shop and livery stable in Clinton. While most of the Taylor men remained on the outskirts of town, Jim Taylor, Mace Arnold (who was known as Winchester Smith) and J. G. Hendrix stabled their horses at King's livery. Meanwhile, Weisiger sent a boy named Charley Page to Cuero to request the assistance of Deputy Sheriff Dick Hudson. Hudson rounded up a posse of Sutton sympathizers which included Kit Hunter (a cousin of the deceased Bill Sutton).

Sheriff Weisiger advised Martin King that a posse was on its way. Weisiger stated that a fight was certain and that King's sons would be in grave danger. The sheriff told him that his sons' lives would be spared if he would agree to help the law by locking up those horses which the Taylor gang had left at his stable. Fearing for the lives of his sons, Martin King agreed to do so.

As the posse rode in, the Taylor men who were in town scampered to reach their horses only to find that they had been locked up. Jim Taylor, Winchester Smith and Hendrix dashed through Martin King's house in an effort to reach a log building situated in an orchard. Suddenly Taylor was confronted by Kit Hunter. Simultaneously, they exchanged shots. Taylor's bullet went through Hunter's hat while Hunter's slug shattered Taylor's right arm. By then, a barrage of bullets were flying at the Taylor men from different directions. Jim Taylor and Winchester Smith were killed. Hendrix was wounded and would soon die. It all happened so fast that those members of the Taylor bunch waiting on the outskirts of town were never able to help. They departed in haste. Martin King's sons were arrested and jailed.

Martin King was a marked man for betraying the Taylors. One night several months later, a volley of gunfire killed Martin King in the

Indianola, Texas, as it looked prior to the hurricane of 1875. The view is looking down Main Street. *Texas State Library & Archives Commission.*

doorway of Dola Davis' Saloon. A slug from the gun of one of the assassins wounded Davis in the leg during the attack.

In early 1876, a posse arrived at the residence of A. J. Allen, a member of the Taylor gang. The Henderson County sheriff advised Allen that they had a warrant for his arrest. Allen refused to submit to arrest, and a fight broke out in which a deputy was killed. Allen was severely wounded and would eventually die. Another man was wounded as well.

Once again, Captain McNelly and his Texas Rangers camped in DeWitt County. Their mere presence minimized trouble.

An incident that was peripheral to the Sutton-Taylor feud occurred on the night of September 19, 1876. Dr. Philip Brassell, a civic-minded citizen, and his son George, a Taylor sympathizer, were forced from their home by a posse—and were then murdered on the road a short distance from their home. Eight posse members were arrested and jailed by the Texas Rangers. Seven members of the posse (which included Bill Cox, a son of Jim Cox) spent years in and out of courtrooms. There were indictments, trials, changes of venue, acquittals, more indictments, more trails, convictions, appeals, more acquittals, another conviction and pardon (and not necessarily in that order). Eventually, all of the accused men walked free.

Bill Taylor remained a fugitive until April 15, 1877, when he was arrested in Coleman by the Texas Rangers. Taylor was taken to the jail at Austin. In late August, he was reunited with John Wesley Hardin. Hardin had been arrested in Pensacola, Florida, on the 23rd of August and was then transported to Austin to await trial for the murder of Sheriff Charles Webb at Comanche. Hardin was found guilty and sentenced to the penitentiary at Huntsville. Bill Taylor was transferred to the jail at Galveston in order to stand trial at Indianola. Following a change of venue to the court at Texanna (which at the time was the county seat of Jackson County), Taylor was acquitted in the killing of Bill Sutton. It was a blow for the prosecution which now asked for a delay in the murder trial of Gabriel Slaughter, obviously with the hope of preparing a better case. A delay was allowed. Taylor was granted a Writ of Habeas Corpus and was able to post bail in the amount of $5,000 which was secured by Bolivar Pridgen, John Taylor, Eugene Kelly and Rice S. Flournoy. Following another continuance, the prosecuting attorney asked for a dismissal of the case. Bill Taylor was a free man.

The bloody Sutton-Taylor feud, which for years had terrorized the citizens of several Texas counties, finally came to an end.

Cullen Baker's Kentucky-style, cap and ball rifle. *Archives Division, Texas State Library*

Chapter Thirteen
Cullen Baker: Fugitive

Cullen Montgomery Baker became an excellent marksman when he was a teenager. At age 18, and a newlywed, Baker killed his first man. He was accused of bullying an orphan by a Cass County, Texas, farmer named Bailey. Baker went to the Bailey farm to seek him out. Bailey, who was on his front porch, fired a shot at Baker as he approached. Baker drew and returned his fire. Baker's first shot connected, and the second hit Bailey in the head. As his horror-stricken family watched, Bailey was dead before he hit the floor. Baker fled to Arkansas, leaving his bride in Texas.

Two years later Baker fatally stabbed a fellow named Wartham. Soon thereafter he traveled to Texas to fetch his wife, whom he brought back to Arkansas. Following the birth of a daughter, Baker's wife died. A couple of years later, in 1862, he remarried and then joined the Army of the Confederate States. Before long he deserted the Confederacy and was on the run again. In fact, he was still in uniform while drinking at a bar in Spanish Bluffs, Arkansas, when four Union soldiers walked in. Baker drew, shot three of the Yankees, and then fled.

Knowing that the Union army attributed the shootings to a Confederate soldier, and realizing that the Confederate army and others were looking for him, Baker decided that the safest place for him to be was in the Union army, so he joined the Federal occupation force. After a little time passed, once again he deserted, this time to join an outlaw gang.

Following the Civil War and the death of his second wife, Baker proposed to her sixteen-year-old sister. Baker's father-in-law, who had grown to detest him, indicated that it would never happen.

A fellow named Rowden owned a country store in Cass County, Texas. Cullen Baker owed him money, and Rowden badgered him to pay his debt. On the evening of June 1, 1867, Baker showed up at the store. He shouted at Rowden to come outside. As Rowden walked through his door with a shotgun in hand, Baker filled him with lead. Rowden dropped dead.

Later that same month, at Pett's Ferry (a place named for the ferry that crossed the Sulphur River), Baker noticed that two soldiers were closely scrutinizing him. They must have recognized Baker, or realized he was a fugitive, for one of them (a sergeant) drew his pistol. Baker also drew and killed the soldier instantly. While the other soldier escaped in one direction, Baker fled in another.

Totally on the run, Cullen Baker relied more and more on robbery for his subsistence. On October 10, 1867, between Boston and Linden, in Cass County, Baker and his new gang of bandits held up a government supply wagon. The wagon was well-protected with four armed guards. When the driver reached for his pistol, Baker fired a shot and killed him. The guards exchanged a few rounds and then fled the scene.

Baker had become a braggart and heavy drinker. In an incident that occurred at Boston, Texas, during October of 1868, Baker took another life. He spotted an army captain named Kirkham and coolly sauntered up to him stating, "I'm Cullen Baker. You looking for me?" Kirkham immediately reached for his gun. Baker shot him through the head. The army captain lurched backwards and fell dead. Once again Baker escaped, but his time was soon to run out.

Thomas Orr, a handicapped school teacher whom Baker had bullied in the past, decided that enough was enough. Accompanied by Baker's second father-in-law and two others, they decided to track Baker until they found him. The group was successful. On January 6, 1869, in southeastern Arkansas, they found Baker and one of his cohorts eating lunch alongside a road. Orr and the others never gave the elusive fugitive a chance. They opened fire with a barrage of shots. Cullen Baker, his companion, and their lunch, all bit the dust.

This photograph of William Preston Longley was made just before his execution at Giddings, Texas, in 1878. *Western History Collections, University of Oklahoma Library.*

Chapter Fourteen
He'll Hang Again, and Again!

While standing on the gallows, on October 11, 1878, at Giddings, Texas, Bill Longley looked around at an audience of hundreds, and stated, "I see a good many enemies around, and mighty few friends." Moments later he dropped through the trap door, but he dropped too far. Within minutes the rope was shortened and Longley was hanged again.

Actually, Longley had been hanged before—eleven years earlier, as a teenager. He had been caught by a posse at the home of a horse thief named Tom Johnson. Johnson and Longley were hanged. Following the lynching, which occurred at the Johnson house, the posse rode off. When the two were cut down, Longley was still alive.

From the days of his youth, William Preston Longley was argumentative, quick-tempered, and a racist, who placed little value on human life—especially those of blacks. About one mile from the Longley farm, near Evergreen, Texas, fifteen-year-old Longley claimed his first victim, a black soldier who was a member of the Reconstruction troops. Longley antagonized the soldier, who was on horseback, into going for his rifle. Longley drew his pistol and fired. The ball struck the soldier's head, and he died instantly. Later that same year (1867) at Lexington, Texas, Longley and a cohort, Johnson McKowen, terrorized a street dance that was being held by a group of blacks. They rode through the festivities, firing several shots. In their wake, they left two dead and several wounded. On another occasion, the following year, three black men had "rubbed" Longley the wrong way. He followed the men to their campsite that was located outside of Evergreen. One of the men shot at Longley as he approached, but was immediately slain by a ball from Longley's pistol. The other two men quickly fled.

The Sutton-Taylor feud, near Yorktown, Texas had gotten out of hand, and Reconstruction troops had been ordered to quell the violence. While working as a cowboy on a nearby ranch, Longley rode into town one day. Mistaking him for one of the Taylor clan, soldiers accosted Longley and a sergeant instructed him to surrender. Believing that they were after him for one of his killings, Longley drew his revolver and discharged a shot at point-blank range. The sergeant toppled from his horse. He was dead. Longley spurred his mount and outraced the pursuing soldiers.

"Wild Bill" Longley briefly rode with Cullen Baker's band of outlaws. After Baker was gunned down in early 1869, Longley joined a cattle drive that was headed for the slaughterhouses in Kansas. It wasn't long before the headstrong trail boss, a fellow named Rector, and the argumentative Longley, began to quarrel. It was all the excuse that Longley needed. He shot the trail boss several times, until his body was motionless.

Bill Longley was always on the run, and while he ran violence followed him everywhere. During a fracas in a Leavenworth, Kansas saloon, he shot another soldier to death. Longley fled the scene by hopping aboard an eastbound freight train. Shortly thereafter, however, he was captured at St. Joseph, Missouri, and subsequently transported back to Kansas and Fort Leavenworth. While behind bars, Longley was able to bribe a military guard who allowed him to escape.

Next, Longley took a job at Camp Brown, Wyoming, as a teamster. Before long, he and a quartermaster named Greggory (possibly Gregory) figured a way to short change the government by miscounting mules, and then selling those that were unreported for a personal profit. Following one sale, Longley split $300 with Greggory. When Greggory found out that the mules had actually sold for $500, he was incensed and set out to find Longley. When Greggory caught up with Longley at a corral, the alert Longley was quicker as his revolver barked once more. Greggory lived through the night and then died. Foolishly,

He'll Hang Again, and Again

Longley made his getaway on a mule, and was easily apprehended. While awaiting transfer from the Camp Brown guardhouse, to serve a thirty-year term at the Iowa State Penitentiary, Longley escaped.

Bill Longley took refuge with the Ute Indians, where he lay low for about a year. By now (1872), he was no longer a teenager. But his age mattered little. He continued the same pattern of murder, run, and then murder again. As he ambled his way back south, Longley mortally wounded a fellow named Charles Stuart during a card game dispute. After returning to Texas, Longley killed another black man, this time because the victim had insulted a white woman. He engaged in a bloody gunfight with a Bell County man named Bill Scrier. Scrier finally died after receiving thirteen wounds in the altercation. On another occasion, Longley armed himself with a shotgun, and then sought out a minister named Roland Lay. Lay was blown away with two blasts of bird shot.

When Bill Longley learned that his cousin, Cale Longley, had been killed by Wilson Anderson, a boyhood friend, he rode to Anderson's farm and executed him with a shotgun blast. Following his arrest in Louisiana, Longley was returned to Texas, where he was tried and sentenced to death for the Anderson murder. While awaiting the gallows at Giddings, Bill Longley wrote to a girl, stating, "Hanging is my favorite way of dying."

Ben Thompson, when he was city marshal at Austin, Texas. *Archives Division, Texas State Library.*

Chapter Fifteen
Vaudeville and Vengeance

  Ben Thompson and John King Fisher, two of the Old West's most notorious gunfighters, met their demise on March 11, 1884, at San Antonio, Texas. Ben had nine wounds and King had thirteen. Ben Thompson supposedly participated in fourteen gunfights. John King Fisher once boasted that he had killed seven men "not counting Mexicans."

  Thompson was a dapper dresser who occasionally attired himself with a long coat, stovepipe hat, and a cane. He was a gambler and former officer of the law. Fisher was a flashy dresser who often wore fringed shirts and crimson sashes. He operated on both sides of a tin star, hiding from it as a renowned rustler, or wearing it (as he was in 1884) as a deputy sheriff from Uvalde. Ben Thompson and John King Fisher were friends.

  This story actually begins in 1880 when Jack Harris and Ben Thompson quarreled over a gambling incident. Harris, Joe Foster and Billy Simms were the owners of a San Antonio hot spot officially known as the Vaudeville Theatre and Gambling Saloon. For two years bitterness built between the men. Foster and Simms also were caught up in Harris' resentment for Thompson. On July 11, 1882, Ben Thompson, who was currently the Austin city marshal, entered the variety theatre. It was obvious that he intended to stir up a ruckus. When he realized that Harris was not there, he exited. Shortly thereafter, Thompson returned and lingered for a while before once again departing. As Ben walked out, Harris entered through another door. An employee advised Harris that Thompson had been "hanging around," and that he sensed trouble. Harris went straight for his shotgun. Meanwhile, Ben had stopped outside the front entrance to speak with Billy Simms, whom he had known for some time. Somebody dashed through the doorway, stating, "Jack has a gun!" As Thompson stepped back toward the front entrance he was confronted by Harris who leveled his weapon. Ben fired quickly, and missed, but his bullet ricocheted and slammed into Harris' chest. Harris turned and staggered up a flight of stairs before he collapsed. Later that night he died. Thompson surrendered to the authorities, was tried and acquitted. Although the incident occurred in San Antonio, he turned in his badge as city marshal of Austin.

In March of 1884, John King Fisher had been in Austin on official business, and wanted to see old friend Ben Thompson before he departed. After visiting several bars together, Ben decided to accompany King as far as San Antonio on King's return trip to Uvalde. A play was appearing at the Turner Hall Opera House which Ben wanted to see. King agreed that they should attend, and the friends left for San Antonio. Later that night, after the play, the two decided to party a little longer. They proceeded on to the Vaudeville Theatre and Gambling Saloon where they had a drink at the bar. The late-night variety show was about to begin upstairs so Fisher and Thompson adjourned to a private box to watch the performance. They were joined by Harris' former partners, Joe Foster and Billy Simms, and a club bouncer named Jacob Coy. Everything was fine until Thompson's conversation turned to Jack Harris' death, at which time Fisher stood, indicating that they should leave before any trouble started. When Foster began to speak, Thompson jammed his six-shooter into the saloon owner's mouth. Coy leaped forward and grabbed the cylinder. Ben withdrew his revolver. Suddenly gunfire erupted. Fisher and Thompson were shot down by a barrage of lead. King was never able to draw, and Ben who already had his pistol in hand, only fired once. Foster was shot in the leg, probably by Thompson's single shot. Joe Foster died following the amputation of his leg. It has always been suspected that the shotgun and rifle fire which felled Thompson and Fisher came from the adjacent box, and the weapons of Canada Bill, a gambler; Harry Tremaine, a vaudeville performer; and a bartender named McLaughlin. Ben Thompson and John King Fisher were too adept with their revolvers to have been massacred in such fashion by the other three occupants of their box.

Dallas Stoudenmire, El Paso city marshal in 1881. *Archives Division, Texas State Library.*

Chapter Sixteen
El Paso's Fighting Marshal

     The early 1880s were turbulent years in the growing border town of El Paso, Texas. City fathers wanted to hire a lawman that would put the "fear of God" into the city's growing criminal element. They wanted a man with a widespread reputation as an expert gunman. They found him. Dallas Stoudenmire was an imposing figure who carried a brace of six-guns under his coat, in leather-lined pockets. He also carried a smaller snub-nosed revolver as a backup weapon. Stoudenmire had fought for the Confederate Army during the Civil War, and several years later was a Texas Ranger. On April 10, 1881, Stoudenmire was sworn in as city marshal of El Paso. Our story, however, begins a few months earlier.

     Prior to the appointment of Dallas Stoudenmire, El Paso had two short-term marshals who would later participate in gunfights with Stoudenmire. Toward the end of 1880, George Campbell served for a few weeks, but received no salary. Campbell assumed that the only way he could endure would be to live off the monies he collected from arrest fees. In an effort to show town officials the importance of his position as city marshal, he persuaded some of El Paso's biggest troublemakers to shoot up the town. They riddled the houses of the mayor and an alderman with bullets. When officials found out that Campbell was behind the trouble, the Texas Rangers were called in. They found the whole matter quite humorous and refused to arrest Campbell. George Campbell was allowed to resign. A former city deputy, Bill Johnson, was appointed as interim marshal. During the months while Johnson served in this capacity, he hoped to receive a permanent commission as El Paso's city marshal. The hiring of Stoudenmire precipitated an unwarranted resentment by Johnson for the new marshal.

Four days after taking office, Stoudenmire was having lunch at the Globe Restaurant (that was owned by his brother-in-law, Doc Cummings) from which he spotted trouble brewing outside on El Paso Street. Tensions had built following the recent murder of two Mexicans, and some Anglos and Mexicans were shouting harsh words at each other. Stoudenmire watched as town constable Gus Krempkau, known to be a friend of the Mexicans, was approached by George Campbell and John Hale. As they quarreled, Hale drew his pistol and shot Krempkau. With his revolvers drawn, Stoudenmire charged out the front door of the Globe Restaurant. He fired a shot at Hale that missed Hale, but accidently hit a Mexican bystander that was scrambling for cover. Stoudenmire's second shot found its mark, striking Hale in the head. Campbell, who was inebriated, had drawn his six-shooter and was waving it around shouting that it wasn't his fight. Krempkau, who was badly wounded and dying, had drawn his revolver and began firing at Campbell. One shot struck him in the wrist, another in the foot. Stoudenmire turned and shot Campbell in the stomach. The shooting stopped. Campbell died the following day, as did the Mexican bystander.

The citizens of El Paso were extremely impressed by the effectiveness of their new city marshal. Some, however, viewed Stoudenmire as a threat. They hatched a plan to dispose of the new marshal, and then enticed Bill Johnson to carry it out. He was happy to do so. Just three days after the shootout with Campbell and Hale, while walking along with his brother-in-law Doc Cummings, Stoudenmire was ambushed by Johnson who was perched high on a pile of bricks at the construction site of the State National Bank. One bullet wounded Stoudenmire in his heel. Stoudenmire and Cummings opened fire on Johnson, pumping eight slugs into his body. Johnson would die. More shots flew toward Stoudenmire from Frank Manning's Saloon. The fighting marshal whirled and charged the saloon with his six-shooters blazing. This act of daring startled the gunmen and they turned and fled. Stoudenmire was certain that the Manning brothers were responsible for the attempt on his life, but he had no proof.

The delight that city officials had for their new city marshal soon turned sour. Dallas Stoudenmire began to drink excessively. Occasionally, when he did so, he would fire his revolvers into the sky, sometimes in the middle of the night. As his alcoholism increased, so did his unfaithfulness to his wife Belle. Under pressure, Stoudenmire resigned his post. He was replaced by a former deputy, shotgun wielding Jim Gillett. Gillett, like Stoudenmire, was a former Texas Ranger and a crack marksman.

The Manning brothers, Doc, Jim, John, and Frank, were a rough bunch. They once vowed that they wouldn't shave until the South rose again. Their feud with Dallas Stoudenmire heightened following an incident in which Jim Manning and David King shot and killed Doc Cummings, after Cummings had belligerently challenged Manning to a fight. Cummings had willed the Globe Restaurant to his brother-in-law, so Stoudenmire assumed the day-to-day chore of operating the eating establishment.

The detestation between Stoudenmire and the Mannings culminated on September 18, 1882, at Frank Manning's Saloon. While Jim Manning was outside looking for his brother Frank, Dallas Stoudenmire forced a showdown with Doc Manning. As they approached each other during heated words, a bystander, J. W. Jones stepped between the two foes. As he was doing so, both men drew their revolvers. Jones was standing in the path of Stoudenmire's gun enabling Manning to get off the first shot. The bullet struck Stoudenmire in the chest and arm causing him to drop his revolver as he reeled backward. Doc Manning grabbed Stoudenmire and the two wrestled their way through the front door and onto El Paso Street. Stoudenmire was able to grasp his snub-nosed revolver, and he pumped a slug into Manning's arm. As the two men continued to grapple, Jim Manning burst on scene with his six-shooter in hand. He fired two shots, the second of which entered Stoudenmire's head behind his left ear. Dallas Stoudenmire, the man who had become a local legend, collapsed and died.

Belton, the county seat of Bell County, as it looked after the Civil War. *Collection of the Bell County Museum.*

Chapter Seventeen
Reprisal in Bell County

During the Civil War there were many communities scattered across the western frontier that lacked adequate protection. While most of the young men were off fighting battles, security was often left to older men and young boys. Sometimes they would organize a protection agency to help guard the home front. Such was the case with the Home Guard in Bell County, Texas. Ethics wasn't a strong suit for many Bell County ranchers. Some used the Home Guard as a screen for rustling activities. On a wide-open range it was easy to round up strays that belonged to neighbors who were on a battlefield far away. Upon returning home, some of the owners would "steal" their cattle and horses back. Much hostility grew out of the rustling activity.

The Home Guard was led by John Early, an individual of dubious character who seemed to enjoy the sport of dragging deserters from their hideouts in the rugged bush country to the west. When the war ended, Early's house became headquarters for scalawags and carpetbaggers. Among his cohorts were Republican Dr. Calvin Clark, considered a turncoat by many, and Judge Hiram Christian, leader of the carpetbaggers. The three men, and their circle of friends, were highly disliked by the majority of Bell County citizens—Southern sympathizers, former soldiers of the Confederate States of America, and their kinfolk.

Sam Hasley was a Confederate soldier who carried a huge grudge against John Early. It began prior to the war's end. In early 1865, John Early and members of the Home Guard captured three deserters who were on the run. Accompanied by their prisoners, the group made camp near a place called Reed's Lake. Two companies of Confederate soldiers also pitched camp nearby. The fugitives were secured before

Early and his bunch retired for the night. The following morning, the Home Guard awoke to find the deserters hanging by their necks from a pecan tree.

Whether, or not, there was any justification in John Early's actions during the aftermath of the hangings is a question which will probably never be answered. Early singled out several locals, went to their homes, quizzed them, badgered them, and then pushed them around. One of the citizens who was on the receiving end was Sam Hasley's father, Drew. Early shoved Drew Hasley around, then jerked a handful of hair from his white beard.

Sam Hasley was not one to rush right into a fight. He was cool, calm, and calculating. When he returned from the war to find that his father had been insulted and mistreated, he vowed retaliation. It was some time before an opportunity arose. One night, while riding on a desolate road, Sam Hasley encountered a group of scalawags who were traveling in the opposite direction. As he passed the column of riders, the white face of the last horse stood out in the moonlight. Hasley realized it was Early's horse. As they neared each other Hasley spurred his mount, fired point-blank at Early, then raced out of sight. When Hasley heeled his mount it caused Early's horse to shy. When it did, Hasley's bullet struck the horse. The horse died and Early was unscathed. Early, Christian and Clark decided that it was time to make an example out of some prominent Southerners in Bell County. He used the lynching of the deserters as an excuse to do so. A detachment of soldiers arrested several people, including Drew Hasley, and escorted them to the jail at Austin. It was the last straw as far as Sam Hasley was concerned.

Lawlessness in Bell County had never been greater. Not only did the authorities take advantage of the citizens, but horse thieves and cattle rustlers were running rampant. The citizens of Bell County finally took matters into their own hands. A group of vigilantes emerged. Their moves were highly calculated and they executed them to precision. Furthermore, they were masters at covering their tracks. The vigilantes moved swiftly. Six previously dreaded outlaws met their demise in April of 1866. In June, the bodies of two more horse thieves were found floating in the river near Three Forks.

Speculation has it that the vigilantes were composed predominately of former Confederate soldiers, and that their leaders were Sam Hasley and his brother-in-law Jim McRae. Whoever they were, their identities were highly protected.

While working at the courthouse on the 2nd of July, Judge Hiram Christian somehow found out that he was a marked man. That night, under the cover of darkness, Christian fled Bell County. The vigilantes tracked him all the way to Missouri, where they finally caught up with him. The execution of Hiram Christian was swift, and the vigilantes returned to Texas.

Jonathan and Newton Lindley departed from San Antonio with a warrant for the arrest of two Bell County men whose names were Duncan and Dawes. They were wanted for the murder of Jasper Lindley, one of the horse thieves who had been found in the river near Three Forks. Jonathan, who was Jasper's father, and Newton were accompanied by fifteen soldiers when they arrived in Bell County. Confident of their innocence, Duncan and Dawes surrendered to the soldiers and the group headed toward San Antonio. Before they had traveled far, Jonathan Lindley shot the two prisoners out of their saddles. He and Newton then fled the scene.

Jonathan and Newton Lindley were captured and escorted to the Bell County jail where they were locked up. While they were awaiting trial, a mob surrounded the jailhouse and then shot and killed the prisoners. Naturally, nobody recognized any members of the mob, nor did anybody "discover" the bodies any time soon.

David Griffin was a brother-in-law of Jim McRae, who, as we have previously mentioned, was a brother-in-law of Sam Hasley. The Hasley, McRae and Griffin clans were suspected as being the core of the vigilantes. While Sam Hasley stepped softly and took a low profile, Jim McRae was bold and blatant, and a more visible leader. McRae had become John Early's number one target. On July 30, 1869, Early and a posse approached the Griffin residence where a party was in progress. The Griffins, McRaes and Hasleys were having a festive time. Fearing that a confrontation would endanger the women and children Early withdrew his men a short distance back down the road. Before long Jim McRae and David Griffin rode up the trail in the direction of the concealed posse members. As the two riders drew near, Early and his men shot McRae out of the saddle. Griffin whirled his mount and fled. The badly wounded McRae was able to discharge a couple of shots and wounded a posse member named McDaniels. Jim McRae died later that evening.

Following McRae's death the vigilantes broke up and dispersed. Eight months later, a telegram was received which announced that "Calvin Clark of Bell County, Texas was killed in Arkansas by a desperado named Halsey [sic] who followed him from Texas."

John Early disappeared. Could he also have met his demise by the hand of Sam Hasley? We may never know.

William Mitchell was determined to attain revenge. *Hood County Museum.*

Chapter Eighteen
The Mitchell-Truitt Conflict

Bill Mitchell was the personification of a tough Texas cowboy. He was a crack marksman and a master with a rope. His leather-beaten face and fine horsemanship were the result of much time spent in the saddle. Bill Mitchell was as imposing an individual as there was in Hood County. He would also become the central figure in the bloody Mitchell-Truitt feud.

William Nelson Mitchell was the seventh child of Nelson "Cooney" Mitchell and his wife Nancy. Bill was born April 16, 1852. Following the Civil War, the Mitchell clan (which consisted of Bill, his parents, two of his brothers and two of his sisters) established a ranch along the Brazos River at a place that would become known as Mitchell's Bend. One day while Bill and Cooney were out rounding up strays they stumbled upon a large family of poor and destitute squatters. It was obvious to the Mitchells that the Truitt family was underfed and needed help. Needing additional hands on his growing ranch, Cooney Mitchell made the Truitts an offer they couldn't refuse. He would help them build a log home and smokehouse and provide them food until they became self-sufficient. In turn, the Truitts would work for the Mitchells. Part of the Truitt's compensation would pay off their indebtedness to the

Mitchells.

Eventually, the Truitts were able to get along without any help. They paid off their debt to the Mitchells (the Truitts at least thought so) and became independent. It wasn't long before they had purchased a piece of property adjacent to Mitchell land. It would be the catalyst for much trouble.

Along the property line where the Truitt land adjoined that of the Mitchells there was a strip which both families claimed to own. Their argument finally wound up in court during March of 1874. The courtroom battle was heated as tempers flew on both sides. The trial (which was ultimately won by the Truitts) aroused a hatred which would quickly turn to violence.

The Truitt boys left the courthouse and had traveled about six miles on their way home when they were confronted by Bill Mitchell, his father, two brother-in-laws and a neighbor. Evidently, the younger Truitts jeered the Mitchells over the outcome of the trial. This action further incensed the Mitchells who opened fire on the Truitts. Sam and Ike Truitt were killed instantly. Jim, the eldest Truitt (who was a minister), was able to take refuge at a nearby house after he was wounded. A few days later Cooney Mitchell, his son-in-law W. J. Owens and their neighbor James Shaw were arrested and charged with murder. Bill Mitchell and his brother-in-law Mitch Graves were able to elude the law

James Morgan Truitt was a minister and newspaperman when he met his demise. *Hood County Museum.*

and became fugitives.

During the ensuing trial, the Reverend Jim Truitt testified against the Mitchells. The jury was convinced that he told the truth. Cooney Mitchell was sentenced to be executed by hanging. Owens and Shaw were also convicted and sentenced to the penitentiary.

One night, while Cooney Mitchell awaited execution, a heavily armed individual attempted to approach the rear of the jailhouse. A guard shot the shadowy figure who toppled down an embankment toward the river. The next morning the body of Jeff Mitchell, Cooney's youngest son, was found. He had been shot through the head.

A crowd gathered for Cooney Mitchell's execution. Before the noose was placed around his neck, Mitchell was asked if he had any last words. Cooney Mitchell called out to his son Bill, wherever he might be, to avenge his father's death. This onus probably didn't make any difference. Bill Mitchell was the kind of individual who would seek revenge anyway.

After the death of Cooney Mitchell the rest of his family left Mitchell's Bend. The Truitts moved on shortly thereafter. Over ten years would pass before Bill Mitchell and Jim Truitt would meet again.

Truitt moved from parish to parish throughout eastern Texas, until he finally wound up at Timpson. There he supplemented his ministry by operating the local newspaper.

Bill Mitchell also moved about during this period. Using the alias of John W. King, Mitchell lived in Fort Stanton, New Mexico, where he worked as a teamster. Although he was not involved in the Lincoln County War, he was there during its worst days. Mitchell returned to Texas and assumed a new alias, John Davis, the name he used when he married Mary Beckett. They lived together, with Mary's father, in an isolated area west of San Antonio. The couple had one child, Maud Jane.

On July 20, 1886, Bill Mitchell rode into Timpson. After receiving directions to the Truitt residence, he walked through the door without knocking. To the horror of Julia Truitt, Jim's wife, and their daughter, Bill Mitchell drew his revolver and shot Jim Truitt through the head. The fugitive then walked outside, mounted his horse and rode away.

It was two full days before Sheriff A. J. Spradley, from Nacogdoches, was summoned and could hit the trail in pursuit of Mitchell. Spradley was not able to track Mitchell very far, so he returned to Timpson.

Twenty-one years passed before Sheriff Swofford of Hood County received a tip that Bill Mitchell was back in Lincoln County, New Mexico, living under his newest alias, Baldy Russell. Swofford and a deputy traveled to New Mexico and located Mitchell. Posing as cattlemen, the lawmen gained his confidence. When the opportunity arose, and Mitchell's guard was down, the lawmen jumped on their prey and handcuffed him. Mitchell was returned to Hood County, Texas, to stand trial for the murders of Ike and Sam Truitt in 1874. An old piece of evidence surfaced which had not been used at Cooney Mitchell's trial. A derringer which belonged to young Ike had one empty chamber. The Mitchells had maintained all along that Ike Truitt fired the first shot. The jury agreed that this was possible, and acquitted Bill Mitchell.

Bill Mitchell was also indicted in the death of Jim Truitt. Mrs. Julia Truitt Bishop, who had remarried and by now was an accomplished writer, traveled from Chicago to identify Bill Mitchell as her ex-husband's murderer. Following a hung jury, the accused was released under a $20,000 bond. Following another hung jury the venue was changed to Cherokee County and once again Bill Mitchell posted bond. He journeyed back to New Mexico from where he furnished sworn affidavits that he was unable to travel to Texas due to illness. His case was continued several times before he finally appeared in court on December 23, 1910. This time he was found guilty, a decision which was upheld two years later by the Court of Criminal Appeals. At the age of sixty-four Bill Mitchell was sent to prison.

After serving just two years of his sentence, Bill Mitchell escaped. Using the alias of John Davis once again, Mitchell eventually settled down in Arizona. At a hospital in San Simon, with Mary at his side, Bill Mitchell died of heart failure on June 26, 1928. He was 76 years old.

McDade, Texas, as it once looked. The building at right is the Rock Saloon. *McDade Historical Museum, Courtesy of Vicki Nisbett.*

Chapter Nineteen
Shootout on Christmas Day

Prior to 1871, McDade, Texas was a sleepy little burg about 34 miles (55 kilometers) east of Austin. That year the Texas Central Railroad arrived and things picked up a bit. A row of brick buildings was constructed, as was a depot right in the middle of town adjacent to the railroad tracks that ran down the main street. The law in Bastrop County was ineffective, as it was in the neighboring counties of Lee and Williamson. The citizens of these three counties were terrorized by a group of rustlers and murderers called the "Notch Cutters," and there was little they could do about it. Occasionally, railroad men were robbed on payday. Ranchers who had sold cattle or horses ran the risk of losing their cash before they could get it to the bank. The Notch Cutters were in the business of selling beef. Rustled, and then butchered cattle could not be identified. It was the Notch Cutters way. Citizens that had the guts to testify against a gang member could be murdered before they ever reached the courtroom. If they were able to testify, in doing so they probably signed their own death warrant. Members of the gang were ranchers themselves scattered throughout the Yegua Creek area of Lee County, in country called the Knobs. Residents of that region, whether respected citizens or not, learned to become excellent marksmen because of constant trouble with the Comanche Indians.

Citizens finally decided to take matters into their own hands and organized a vigilance committee. Nobody knows for certain when it started or who the original organizers were, but it most likely began sometime in late 1873 or early 1874, in McDade. Naturally, the identities of those involved needed to remain a secret. The first "conviction" by the vigilantes was probably on May 4, 1874. The bullet-riddled body of a negro who had killed a white man was found hanging from a tree on that date. Two fellows named Waddell and Land, who were believed to be members of the Notch Cutters, were hanged side-by-side in January of 1875.

The Notch Cutters retaliated. Businessman Horace Alsup had traveled to Lexington, in Lee County, for a work related meeting. On his return trip, he was blasted from his saddle by a shotgun. Twelve slugs were found in his body. Bill Craddock had been an eye witness to cattle rustling. Furthermore, he recognized the culprits and went to court to testify against them. Soon thereafter, while on his way home from a days work at the syrup mill, he was also shotgunned to death. Later, another hanging occurred. A fellow named Howard Cordell, who was part Indian, was hanged (possibly by the vigilantes). Supposedly, it was said that Cordell was a "hereditary horse thief."

One of the larger spreads to have suffered a great deal of cattle rustling was the Olive Ranch in Williamson County, just across the line from Bastrop County. It was operated by the Olive brothers, Jay, John, Prentice, and Jim. On March 22, 1876, on their ranch, somebody discovered skinned and dressed beef, but nobody was around. It is believed that they were sure the rustlers would return for the goods and took cover to await their return. When the rustlers finally appeared, they were gunned down by the men in hiding. The two dead rustlers, James H. Crow and Turk Turner, were left on the prairie. One of Crow's sons departed from his home to search for his father when the latter did not return. Young Crow found the bodies. It is uncertain who did the shooting for there were no other witnesses. The Olive brothers were blamed. When the case went to court, it was quickly dismissed for lack of evidence.

During the evening on August 1, 1876, a large group of Notch Cutters attacked the Olive Ranch. A bloody battle ensued in which Jay and Prentice Olive were seriously injured, as were two of the ranch hands. The ranch house was torched but the glow from the flames made the outlaw gang easy targets. Blood of the attackers was found in several spots the following morning, but the number of outlaw casualties is unknown.

One day two men were found hanging near the Williamson County line. They were both dressed in fine clothes and were carrying a large sum of money that seemed to be untouched. Neither had any identification and nobody in the area had ever seen them before. Later, another dead man was found, naked, lying on a blanket. He was never identified either. No inquiries ever surfaced regarding the unknown dead men. Strange things were known to happen around McDade.

Pat Erhart was a music teacher and bachelor who lived in a settlement called Blue in the Knobs area. He was liked by everyone. Periodically he would host a party and dance at his large home and people would come from throughout the region to partake in the festivities. One of Erhart's parties took place on June 27, 1877. It was mandatory for all guests to check their firearms when they arrived in order to avoid any trouble. At approximately 2 a.m., a group of masked vigilantes surrounded the house. They presented Erhart with a list of five names of the men they wanted to see. The list read Wade Alsup, John Kuykendall, Young Floyd, Beck Scott, and Jim Floyd. All of the men responded with the exception of Jim Floyd. The vigilantes bound the wrists of the four men with rawhide, placed them on horses, and then led them down the road a piece where they were hanged. The lynchings seemed to have an effect on the Notch Cutters because violence was minimal for several years thereafter.

Storekeeper George Milton, who we now know was deeply involved with the vigilantes, was in his place of business on August 23, 1883, when a lad named Bob Young stepped through the front door and fired his shotgun at Milton. Young missed, and then fled. The persistent fellow returned the following day and missed again. This time Milton gunned him down. Two more murders occurred nine miles (14 kilometers) from McDade on November 22, 1883. In the small settlement of Fedor, a storekeeper named Keffel and his clerk were robbed and killed.

While returning from a business trip to Bastrop, Allen Wynn was accosted by members of the Notch Cutters who shot him, robbed him, and then left thinking he was dead. Wynn, who was a partner of George Milton and Thomas Bishop in both the cattle and saloon business, played dead after a bullet wounded him superficially. Although he was losing blood, he was able to drive his buckboard home and then send for Milton and Bishop. Wynn informed them that he had recognized his assailants. This mistake by the Notch Cutters would cost them dearly.

A few days later, during the evening on December 1, 1883, Deputy Sheriff Isaac Heffington of Lee County was in McDade trying to follow up on the murders in Fedor. The lawman was shot in the chest at close range near the edge of town. His attacker fled. Heffington would die shortly thereafter. This renewed activity by the Notch Cutters raised the ire of the vigilantes. It was time for them to go back into action.

At about 7:30 p.m., on Christmas Eve, 1883, eight masked

vigilantes entered the Rock Saloon in McDade, four through the front door and four through the rear door. They stuck their weapons into the guts of Thad McLemore, Wright McLemore, and Henry Pfeiffer. Thad McLemore was one of the men that had been identified by Allen Wynn. The trio had their hands tied behind their backs and were led down the road about a mile (1.6 kilometers) where they were hanged.

Christmas morning found Thomas Bishop, George Milton, and Dr. Vermillion sitting on the porch in front of George Milton's store. Down the street several people were celebrating the holiday at the Rock Saloon. Six men who were related by marriage rode in together and were also having a good time at the Rock Saloon until they were informed that the vigilantes had hanged three of their friends the night before. Jack, Heywood, and Asbury "Az" Beatty, Charley Goodman, Byrd Hasley, and Robert Stevens were shaken by the news. In the conversation that followed, Jack Beatty claimed that Milton and Bishop had accused Heywood Beatty of assisting in the death of Heffington, the deputy sheriff. Furthermore that he intended to kill both of them. Jack Beatty was advised that both Milton and Bishop were sitting on the front porch of Milton's store at that very moment. The six men concocted a quick plan and decided that it was time right then to rid themselves of both Milton and Bishop. Jack Beatty approached George Milton and reminded him that he (Beatty) had $35 on deposit and would like to get his money. Milton agreed and the two entered the store. It was part of the gang members' plan to split Milton and Bishop. While Milton was inside, Bishop was confronted by Az Beatty on the front porch. Az went for his gun, but Bishop beat him to it and fired a shot that hit Az Beatty in the thigh. The two grappled and rolled into the street. When Milton heard the shot he quickly got the drop on Jack Beatty. Bishop fired again and Az Beatty dropped dead. Milton then grabbed his shotgun as he herded Jack Beatty out the front door and into the street. Byrd Hasley and Charlie Goodman were just outside. Gunfire continued with Goodman taking a slug and falling wounded in the street. Hasley fled the scene. Robert Stevens was also wounded. Jack Beatty was shot in the head by both a pistol and a shotgun blast. He was also dead. Willie Griffin ran out of the Rock Saloon and took a bullet in the head from the pistol of Heywood Beatty. Heywood Beatty had been hit several times, but was able to crawl off between buildings and fled to his home and a doctor's care. Both of his brothers were dead, but he would survive. Willie Griffin died the next day. George Milton and Thomas Bishop were unscathed during the battle. They were arrested, as were Goodman and Stevens. All were released on bond. Governor Ireland ordered the Texas Volunteer Guard to McDade to establish order. The fight was already over so they encountered no difficulty.

During a citizens meeting on December 27, 1883, a list of names was established of undesirables. Those people named on the list were given ten days to either leave the region or stay and be hanged. Henceforth the Notch Cutters were nonexistent.

Temple Houston, while he was a district attourney at Mobeetlie, Texas. *Archives Division, Texas State Library.*

Chapter Twenty
Orator, Lawyer, Sharp-Shooter

Temple Lea Houston was the youngest son of renowned Texas patriot Sam Houston and his wife Margaret Moffette (Lea). His birth was on August 12, 1860, and he was the first child born in the governor's mansion at Austin. The infant was named for his maternal grandfather, Temple Lea, a Baptist minister. He grew to become one of the Southwest's most brilliant criminal lawyers. He was eloquent, flamboyant and fearless – and was one of the most accurate marksmen on the western frontier. A journalist once described Temple Houston as "a gun-toting, tough hombre and silver-tongued darling of the frontier courtroom, who spouted French and Spanish fluently, spoke seven Indian tongues, quoted Greek scholars, the Bible and Shakespeare, and died with his boots on." Houston did not fit the mold of a typical gunfighter, and he wasn't. He was a most interesting person who just happened to be involved in a couple of skirmishes with firearms. Although a native Texan, he eventually moved to Oklahoma.

On February 14, 1883, Temple married the beautiful and aristocratic Laura Cross. He moved Laura, who was reared on a plantation, to the rowdy town of Mobeetie in the Texas panhandle. The couple had several children, Temple Jr., Louise (who died young), Sam, Mary Lea and Richard. Laura once said of Temple, he was, "one of the gentlest men I've ever known. When he was reading a paper or book and I spoke of something, no matter how busy he was, he would lay his book or paper aside and become interested in what I had to say. When I would fly up and lose control of myself, he would call me his 'handful of powder on a red-hot stove'."

According to El Reno, Oklahoma attorney Colonel Robert S. Forrest, "No man had a finer control of the English language... in sympathetic appeals he developed remarkable force. The heart-stricken wife, the weeping and aged mother, the fatherless child, the disappointed and inconsolable sweetheart – whatever the object of distress, he could touch a heart of stone in painting its sorrows." Houston served two terms as senator in the Texas State Legislature during the years 1885 to 1889. On May 16, 1888, Temple Houston gave the dedicatory oration for the newly constructed Texas State Capitol at Austin. Politics wasn't Temple's game, however. He didn't want to be tabbed as following in his father's footsteps. He loved the excitement of a courtroom and the bustle of frontier towns like Mobeetie.

Temple Houston dressed eccentrically. He was often seen in a black frock coat, a yellow-beaded vest, satin-striped trousers, shop-made boots of the finest leather, topped off with a white Stetson hat. Beneath his coat, in a tooled leather holster, he carried "Old Betsy," the pearl-handled Colt revolver that helped make him legendary. A tale has been passed down through the years about an incident that allegedly took place at nearby Tascosa. Bat Masterson reportedly arranged a shooting match between Temple Houston and Billy the Kid. Supposedly, the tin star trademark was removed from a package of chewing tobacco and tacked up on a post. Temple drew and fired hitting the center of the star with deadly accuracy. Billy said, "Quien lo haja major?" (Who could do better?), chuckled and departed. Either the incident is pure fiction, or it never happened at Tascosa. When Temple Houston arrived at Tascosa for the first time, Billy the Kid had been dead for ten months. The tale accurately reflected Houston's marksmanship, however.

Houston wasn't much of a card player and he seldom gambled unless it was on a shooting match in which he was a participant. On holidays or special occasions when such matches were part of the festivities, Temple might be seen in a beautifully tailored buckskin outfit, with his auburn hair sweeping his shoulders beneath a wide-brimmed Mexican sombrero. Onlookers who watched Houston and "Old Betsy" score one bulls-eye after another were certain that he could outshoot any gunfighter on the frontier. On one occasion, Houston was challenged by a woman, Mobeetie's Mollie Quillin, who was an excellent marksman herself. She would hunt deer and antelope with male companions and bag more game than the men. A nickel was wedged into a crack atop a fence rail. Mollie shot first and hit the nickel – on its edge. The nickel was again placed on the rail and Temple leveled his pearl-handled revolver and fired. His bullet struck the very center of the coin. Mollie saved the nickel as a souvenir until she passed away in 1940.

Many stories are told about Temple Houston's eloquence and theatrics within the courtroom, both in Texas and Oklahoma. While defending a soiled maiden from Canadian, Texas, against a charge of prostitution, Houston declared that, "Where the star of purity once glittered on her girlish brow, burning shame has set its seal forever," and he asked the jury to let her "go in peace." They obliged. Miss Stacy credited the change in her life to Houston's plea. Years later, following Temple's death, she would send her condolences to his family with a batch of wild prairie flowers.

Temple Houston once defended a cowboy who was charged with stealing a horse and killing the animal's owner. The prosecution wanted the alleged killer to hang. Temple maintained that the murdered man was a skilled gunfighter and that the defendant had acted in self-defense. Houston stated, "This malefactor was so adept with a six-shooter that he could place a gun in the hands of an inexperienced man, then draw and fire his own weapon before his victim could pull the trigger. Like this!" In a flash, Houston drew "Old Betsy" and fired several shots point blank at the jury. Judge McAtee ducked beneath his bench, while the jurors scattered throughout the courtroom. Houston, who had already holstered his revolver, innocently looked about. "Your Honor," he chuckled, "you need not have been afraid. My cartridges were all blanks… I only wanted to show what speed this dead man possessed." The alarmed jury, possibly feeling that they had been made fools of, found the cowboy guilty anyway. Temple Houston immediately filed a motion for a retrial on the basis that, following his volley of blanks, the jury had "separated during the hearing and mingled with the crowd," and therefore had not been sequestered. The judge admitted that the strict rule of procedure had been violated. At a new trial a few months later the cowboy was acquitted.

Deputy U.S. Marshall, Chris Madsen, operating from El Reno, Oklahoma, arrested Alfred Son for the murder of Fred Hoffman, treasurer of Dewey County and district U.S. commissioner. Hoffman had been killed on January 22, 1895, by a bullet through the neck. Alfred Son was in the proximity, as was an unidentified man on a gray horse. Following two long and complex trials, Alfred Son was found guilty and sentenced to life in prison. When Houston's motion for a new trial was overruled, he appealed to the Oklahoma Supreme Court and a new trial was granted. The Alfred Son affair was representative of Houston's persistence, fearlessness and his silver-tongued oratory. The man on the gray horse turned out to be "Red Buck" George Weightman, a former member of Bill Doolin's Oklahombres, who was using the alias of Bert Collins. Son was afraid to testify against Collins (Weightman) for fear of his life. Houston received a message from Weightman, requesting a meeting on a certain night at a remote location. The note further asked Houston to come alone and unarmed. Temple did so. The outlaw, who was armed, told Houston, "I killed Hoffman and don't want another man taking credit for my crime." He was saying that he didn't want Son to suffer for his crime. Houston informed Weightman that his responsibility was only to defend Alfred Son, not to accuse someone else. Houston held the meeting in confidence and did not mention it to anyone until after Weightman was shot to death at Arapahoe, Oklahoma on February 14, 1896. When the U.S. Federal Court for the Second District convened for the November, 1897 session, Alfred Son's retrial was on the docket. The courtroom was jammed. Houston reviewed the evidence, then expounded on an eloquent discourse directed straight at the jury. To quote only a portion of his remarks would be an injustice.

Houston stated, "Gentlemen, as I told you in the beginning, the Territory has shown no motive for the commission of such a crime and we have given you a reasonable – a true – explanation of every act and utterance of the defendant – even for his trip that fatal direction. He went to woo – and win – one of the daughters of the land, tender-eyed, fair to look upon; and how like a boy, to make the shortest route to see his sweetheart, and, seeing her, take her back by the longest. The life of this boy, up to the instant of his accusation, has been faultless; and do you believe that he took the sudden and awful plunge from innocence into fathomless depths of crime – from child-like purity into hideous murder?

When asked to believe such a supposition, refer to your duties as given you in His Honor's charge; apply the law as there laid down to the proof and then follow the dictates of your conscience, and I do not fear the result.

This brave boy asked me to say to you that, to him, honor is clearer than life, and as the old exemplar of purest patriotism thundered in the ears of his country's oppressors, he says in this, his hour of trial, "give me liberty or give me death." He demands that you free him or inflict the death penalty. Rather than that you should fix upon his boyish brow the brand of felon, he would prefer to walk from your presence with his body polluted with the scales of whitest leprosy. He appeals to no sentiment of pity; only to the injustice of his country's laws, which you are so solemnly charged to administer.

You came into that box with light hearts and consciences clear. Oh, may you leave there thus! Untortured with the curse of having wrecked the life of him whose life you hold in the hollow of your hands. And he is so young, too. Boyhood's down still softens upon his childlike face. You will not be here long now. Your homes where loved ones are even now watching, waiting. To greet you, and when you clasp them to your manly breasts may the rapture at the moment be not embittered by the memory of having wrecked the life of yonder boy, whom all law and righteousness plead with you to save.

Gentlemen, be just; heed not the perjured friends who thirst for this boy's blood, and in the years yet to come, when the pale messenger summons you before the court where you shall be tried alongside the kings of earth, each memoried hour of life shall come back to you with awful distinctness, then happily can you recall that when you judged here, you judged with justice, and in the very spirit of Him who said: "Even as you did it to the least of these, so you did it unto me." So that in the perfection of righteousness you tried the stranger within your gates – for he never saw one of you until he fearlessly placed his fate in your hands – even as you would be tried yourselves.

He has a Texas home far across the southern prairies, where the skies are a deeper purple, where the dawn has a brighter glow and the sunset wears a softer gold; where midnight stars look down upon us in a more unspeakable splendor. His loved ones, like yours, are waiting – no! no! not like yours – for his life is darkened even now by the awful shadow of death; and who shall tell what he feels?

Gentlemen, break that suspense; dry those tears; bind up these almost broken hearts, for now no power but you can do so. This noble duty done, each hour of life thereafter will grow proud with this recollection!" The jury deliberated, and then found Alfred Son not guilty.

October 8, 1895, was a fateful day at Woodward, Oklahoma. Temple Houston had squabbled with two attorneys, brothers Ed and John Jennings. Ed Jennings had questioned the admissibility of certain testimony in a court case. Houston suggested that Jennings "must be grossly ignorant of the law." Ed Jennings exploded, slamming his fist on the table, and then lunged toward Houston in an effort to slap his face. Others present jumped between the two and tempers cooled for the moment. Judge J.D.F. Jennings (father of Ed and John) reportedly reprimanded his sons that evening for the incident. The judge and another son, Al, who was also an attorney, headed home for the night leaving Ed and John still working at the office. Temple Houston and Jack Love, a former sheriff, had adjourned to Jack Garvey's Cabinet Saloon and were having a few drinks in the gambling room to the rear. After a while, the Jennings brothers stepped into the saloon and ordered a drink at the bar. As they stared at the others in the back room, they slightly rotated their gun belts for better position. Temple rose from his chair and called out, "Ed, I want to see you a minute." Ed's retort was, "See me here and now you son of a b****!" – and he drew. Houston was faster and his shot struck Ed Jennings in the head and blew away a piece of his skull. Almost simultaneously, a bullet from Love's six-shooter crashed into John Jennings' arm. The concussion created by the first shots put out the saloon lights. More shooting occurred in the darkness, but all the damage had been done. It was later discovered that another bullet hit Ed Jennings in the back of his head, which most likely came from his own brother's gun in the darkness. Both Temple Houston and Jack Love were charged with first degree manslaughter, and then released under $5,000 bonds. Telegrams and letters poured in from all over Texas and Oklahoma supporting Houston, a reflection of the high esteem in which he was held. Most of the witnesses of the gunfight testified that Houston and Love had clearly fired in self-defense. Both were acquitted. Al Jennings swore he would kill Houston – a threat which never came to pass.

Another incident occurred approximately one year later. Temple had just given his son Sam a fine new pony. Now owning any pasture land, Temple suggested that Sam ask a local farmer, J. B. Jenkins if he would mind letting Sam's pony graze on his land. When Sam inquired of the farmer, Jenkins evidently felt he was being taken advantage of and spat in the boy's face. After informing his father of the incident, Temple went looking for the ill-mannered scoundrel. He encountered Jenkins in front of Cattle King Hotel. Both men reached for their six-shooters. Once again, "Old Betsy" barked first. Houston's first slug tore into Jenkins' chest and shoulder. His right arm was ripped by the second slug. Renowned as a deadly marksman, Houston had no trouble convincing authorities that he only meant to maim Jenkins – and that he did so in self-defense. He was charged with "unlawful shooting," a misdemeanor to which he pled guilty and paid a fine.

From the time he moved to Oklahoma, Temple Houston continually resisted the efforts of Democratic Party officials to recruit him for one office or another. Although he had removed himself from a political career in his native Texas, Houston remained abreast of party activities. He once dispatched the following poem to a Dallas newspaper after learning that the State Democratic Convention had adjourned after days of disagreement over candidates and a platform:

> Out on the marge of a moonlit strand
> The whing-whang sits with his tongue in the sand,
> And writes his name with his tail on the land
> And rubs it out with his ogreish hand.

Is it the voice of guns or geeks,
Or what is the voice the whing-whang seeks
As he prowls around midst winding creeks,
And holds his breath for weeks and weeks?

During the early weeks of 1905, Temple Houston had become ill. Streptococcus had infected his bloodstream, and general pyemia had set in. For months he had spasmodic convulsions, became partially blind and paralyzed. A brain hemorrhage on August 15, 1905, relieved him of his misery. With friends and admirers from near and far, and the entire population of Woodward at hand, Temple Lea Houston was laid to rest.

The *Oklahoma State Capital* reflected on Houston stating that he was "by profession a lawyer, incidentally a scholar of aesthetics and classics, by accident a pioneer, and by nature a fighter. ... Oklahoma should inscribe in her book of records a paragraph to one of her most forceful, if not one of her most effective pioneers." In expressing regrets, the *Dallas Times-Herald* observed that Temple was, "a chip off the old block, he had great gifts and strong passions. The Gods were kind to him – he was not kind to himself. Eloquent as an orator, able as a lawyer, and frank and engaging as a comrade, he should have won renown in the law and politics in the state of his nativity, but…he cast his lot with Oklahoma." Twenty-five years after his death, Temple Houston became the model for the character Yancey Cravat when Edna Ferber penned her epic novel *Cimarron*.

San Augustin Church in Laredo faces San Augustin Plaza circa 1880. *Webb County Heritage Foundation*.

Chapter Twenty-One
Laredo: The Botas and Guaraches

Colonel Santos Benavides was a Confederate war hero of legendary status who had established a political base in Laredo by the end of the Civil War. Dario Gonzales served under Benavides during the war. They were friends and fixtures in the Democratic Party. Gonzales was elected sheriff of Webb County in the election of 1872. The Democratic Party split that year as a result of many election irregularities. Leading the anti-Benavides faction was a wealthy businessman, Raymond Martin. Martin, a Frenchman, had opened a general store east of San Augustin Plaza and had acquired much land in Webb County. Much of his property was purchased, while some of it was seized from farmers and ranch owners who defaulted in their loans. Gonzales switched his allegiance and was reelected sheriff in 1876 as a Martin supporter. By the 1880s the Martin group virtually controlled Laredo and Webb County politics.

Santos Benavides, the banking brothers Daniel and Patricio Milmo, and J. J. Haynes, a prominent Republican, led a reform movement. They adopted the guarache (the sandal) as their emblem, significant as the symbol of the "common man." Not to be outdone, the Martin faction chose the F (the boot) as their trademark. Each faction now had a name: the Botas and the Guaraches. Both political parties held lectures, parades, and demonstrations to solicit supporters and intimidate the other party.

Dario Gonzales and Raymond Martin had a falling out in 1883. Supposedly, Gonzales had collected more than $2,000 in taxes from Encinal County (now the western portion of Webb County) which was within his jurisdiction. The money never reached the county treasury. Gonzales was sued and fired as sheriff. When the matter reached the Texas Supreme Court, Gonzales was exonerated. He blamed Martin for his debacle and once again joined the group now known as the Guaraches. Dario Gonzales would soon become the leader of the Guaraches.

The Botas swept the 1884 elections, and the hatred by each faction for the opposite party grew. Two years later, on election day, April 6, 1886, with animosity at its peak, the Botas won again, but this time the Guaraches were able to win two seats on the city council. They were making inroads, they thought, and decided to celebrate their small victory. They dug up one of two Civil War cannons that had been partially buried with its muzzle down (it was being used as a hitching post). The Guaraches painted it yellow and fired it on the evening of the 6th as part of their celebration. The partying by the Guaraches infuriated the Botas who decided to hold a funeral procession to bury the Guarache in effigy. Gonzales was angry. He advised his cohorts that he would allow the Botas to parade, but not to bury the Guarache in effigy. Furthermore he was quoted as saying that "someone else was going to be buried."

The Bota funeral procession began at Bota Hall at 3 p.m. on the afternoon of April 7th and was to proceed to the home of Dario Gonzales where a symbolic sandal would be dramatically buried. The funeral cortege included 30 armed horsemen and 120 riflemen on foot. Additionally, the Botas had snipers stationed at various vantage points to protect the route of the two-block long procession. The Guaraches set up a blockade in front of the Botas with their yellow cannon and armed partisans. Somebody squeezed off a shot, and all hell broke loose. It is estimated that in the next thirty minutes some 2,000 rounds were fired. The cannon's fuse was lit and the old weapon blasted a barrel full of nails which did no damage to anything except the church at San Agustin Plaza. Nobody knows for certain how many casualties resulted from the melee. The best estimate might be sixteen dead and scores wounded. Some bodies were dumped into the Rio Grande River and some of the wounded struggled across the border into Mexico. Eight funerals were held on the very day following the shooting.

Botas claimed that a Guarache, Francisco Garcia, fired the

first shot. Guaraches claimed that the first shot was fired by a Botas, Concepcion Hererra. The bloodbath in Laredo is another episode during a very violent period in Texas history. By the time the election of 1890 arrived, the Guaraches nearly ceased to exist.

Texas Rangers, Company "E," at Alice, Texas in 1892.
Archives Division, Texas State Library.

Chapter Twenty-Two
The Corps of Rangers

The Texas frontier consisted of vast areas of very low population density. The acute problems of law enforcement, or lack thereof, necessitated a high degree of self reliance from ordinary citizens. Mexican authorities offered very little assistance in alleviating the Indian threat. English speaking settlers learned to fend for themselves. As colonists formed communities, some established their own small "militia," which amounted to little more than a patrol to scout the nearby plains. They were often called "Rangers."

During the days of the Republic of Texas, Rangers performed more like soldiers than law enforcement officers. The Plans and Powers of the Provisional Government of Texas (1835, Of the Military, Article IX) provided that, There shall be a corps of Rangers under command of a major, to consist of one hundred and fifty men, to be divided into three or more detachments, and which shall compose a battalion, under the Commander-in-chief when in the field.

By 1840, under Captain John C. Hays, the group (armed with new Colt revolvers) achieved a more permanent status. They remained a quasi-military unit, however, which lacked discipline and had a reputation for bloodthirsty conduct.

During the 1850s, a Ranger collected wages of $25 per month. He provided his own horse, saddle, blankets, pistol and knife. There were no uniforms. Every four days, he would receive rations of flower, rice, sugar, coffee, hard bread, bacon, pork and sometimes beef. Additionally, he would receive a bushel of corn and hay for his horse.

Ranger activity decreased during the Civil War. In 1865, Governor Andrew J. Hamilton issued a proclamation which made a civil, rather than military, force out of the Texas Rangers. The Rangers were asked to act in areas where civil authorities were inadequate to correct lawlessness. Governor Hamilton empowered the chief justice of those counties where violence and disorder were rampant and where other such acts were anticipated, to appoint a captain, and organize (at the expense of the county) a company of Rangers. Each company would consist of between ten and fifty men which would act as a special police force.

In 1870, in an effort to provide adequate statewide security, a new organization called the Texas State Police was formed. It was a highly unpopular force, which had no bounds to limit its sometimes oppressive nature. The unit was abolished by the legislature, in 1873, and the Texas Rangers rode once again.

The Texas Rangers of the late 19th Century were generally tough young men who demonstrated ability, yearned for excitement, and had a desire to uphold the law. They normally wore rough clothing – often buckskin. Most wore broad-brimmed sombreros and vests (much like the Mexican cowboys or vaqueros) and short coats (during colder weather) so they could maneuver with ease while in the saddle. Rarely did a Ranger wear a badge, and when one did it was made for the Ranger at his own expense (usually fashioned from a five-peso coin). They rode a good horse, carried a carbine, pistol and plenty of ammunition.

Texas Rangers worked as a border patrol along the Rio Grande, helped to control problems which arose between Indians and white men, and assisted local law enforcement and private police forces (such as those of the railroads and livestock industry) to quell acts of violence, disorder and other lawlessness. They also conducted criminal investigations, were used as special guards and even collected taxes. Texas Rangers assisted in many notable cases during the nineteenth century. The most famous of those being the killing of Sam Bass and the capture of John Wesley Hardin.

The Rangers were a formidable force as lawmen throughout Texas. They created legends, often as a result of overstepping their bounds. It was not unusual for Rangers to bring a fugitive in dead (when often it wasn't necessary) because he may have been a highly wanted man or because he may have displayed immunity from certain local courts. They were also known to have illegally chased their prey on several occasions across the border into Mexico. Although the Rangers were effective in enforcing the law, the means and methods which they used sometimes resulted in trials in order to defend charges of misconduct. Indictments for misconduct continued well into the twentieth century.

The Texas Rangers were the most feared law enforcement agency on the American frontier. The organization was the oldest state law enforcement agency in the country, as well. Their image has endured. It must be remembered, however, that the bulk of police activity in Texas remained with the local agencies, at a city or county level. Some areas of Texas didn't desire or require Ranger service.

Ira Aten and his Texas Rangers attempted to intercede during the hostilities of August 16, 1889. Aten later became sheriff of Fort Bend County. *Fort Bend Museum.*

Chapter Twenty-Three
Ira Aten: Lawman

Ira Aten, was born in Illinois on September 3, 1862, the second of four sons of Austin and Kate Aten. The family relocated to a farm near Round Rock, Texas, in 1876. Ira spent his teenager years there near the famed Chisholm Trail where the great cattle drives once made their way north to the railheads in Kansas. At age 15, Ira was in Round Rock when the outlaw Sam Bass was mortally wounded in July of 1878. Bleeding profusely, Bass was brought into town by a railroad crew for medical attention. Among those who attended to him was Ira's father, a Methodist minister.

Ira Aten was an excellent marksman and joined the Texas Rangers at the age of twenty. His first assignment as a member of Company D was duty along the Mexican border. He was stationed at Camp King, near Uvalde, under the command of Captain Lamar P. Sieker. In May of 1884, Aten distinguished himself near the Rio Grande River about 80 miles southeast of Laredo. He and six other Rangers were in pursuit of a gang of cattle rustlers when they spotted two of the outlaws. Ira and two other Rangers rode hard to catch the culprits before they crossed the border into Mexico. Both of the other Rangers were wounded in the chase. Firing his rifle, while still on his mount, Aten inflicted wounds on both of the bandits. For his heroics, Ira Aten was promoted to the rank of corporal.

In what became known as the Fence Cutting War of 1886, many ranchers closed off the open range by installing fences around their land. This irritated drovers who were accustomed to driving their cattle across the open range. Some simply cut the fences and herded their cattle across private property. Aten placed hidden dynamite charges along certain fence lines. When the fence was cut, the dynamite would explode. Word quickly spread about the charges, and the fence cutting was substantially reduced. The Adjutant General disapproved of the measure and ordered the charges removed, but because of the uncertainty involved far fewer fences were cut even after the charges were uprooted.

Ira Aten set out on the trail of Judd Roberts, a murderer who had escaped from the San Antonio jailhouse. In April of 1887, Aten surprised Roberts at a ranch near the county line between Williamson and Burnet counties. From a hidden vantage point Aten attempted to capture Roberts as he rode up to the ranch house. Roberts drew and fired wildly at Aten, who returned the fire. Roberts was hit in his hand and dropped his pistol, but he was able to spur his horse and make good his escape.

Two months later while Aten was back in Williamson County he spent the night at the ranch of John R. Hughes in Liberty Hill who also had issues with Roberts. Not realizing that Aten was there, Roberts crept up to the Hughes ranch house the following morning with the intention of killing John Hughes. Once again, Aten attempted to arrest Roberts, but as before the culprit escaped. Aten convinced Hughes to join forces with him, and the two set out in pursuit of the escaped convict. After trailing Roberts for close to one month, the manhunters finally cornered him at a ranch in the Texas panhandle. The fugitive had been courting the ranch owner's daughter. Roberts tried again to shoot his way to freedom, but was gunned down by six bullets from the firearms of Aten and Hughes. Judd Roberts died in the arms of his weeping girlfriend. Ira Aten convinced John Hughes to join the ranks of the Texas Rangers, which he did the following month in August of 1887. Hughes went on to become a distinguished and long-time member of the law enforcement agency.

Near Vance, Texas, in December of 1889, Ira Aten, John Hughes, fellow Ranger Bass Outlaw, and Deputy Sheriff Will Terry set a trap for rustlers and accused murderers Alvin and Will Odle. The ambush occurred in the evening on a moonlit night. The brothers were shot from their saddles by a barrage of bullets from the guns of the lawmen, and they both died instantly.

Governor Lawrence S. Ross sent Sergeant Ira Aten to Richmond, Texas, in Fort Bend County, to quell the political Jaybird-Woodpecker feud. He, and his detachment of eight Texas Rangers, were able to prevent further bloodshed for a while, but were unable to help when a major battle ensued in August of 1889. Once matters cooled down, Aten was elected as the new sheriff of Fort Bend County.

Within a few months, Ira moved to a homestead near Dimmitt, Texas, in Castro County, where he became involved in an election controversy with two brothers Hugh and Andrew McClelland. Andrew, who was seeking election as county judge, called Ira a liar. Once the election was over and McClelland was defeated, Aten sought him out to settle up for the insult. When Aten approached and found Andrew McClelland unarmed he advised the defeated candidate to arm himself. McClelland went to a nearby store and returned with a new .45 in each hand. After firing two wild shots at Aten, the former Texas Ranger coolly shot McClelland in the arm knocking him off his feet. Aten allowed friends of the wounded man to carry him off, when a shot rang out from another direction. Aten saw that the shooter was Hugh McClelland who ducked behind a nearby shack. Aten fired through the flimsy planks wounding the McClelland brother twice. Hugh McClelland wisely fled the scene.

Ira married Imogen Boyce in Austin on February 3, 1892, and brought her to his home in Dimmitt. The couple subsequently had three sons and two daughters. In 1895 Ira was hired by the Capitol Syndicate Company to put a stop to cattle rustling on the XIT Ranch. Aten organized a ranch police force of twenty cowboys that included two former Texas Rangers. All were armed with Winchester rifles.

In 1904 Ira Aten moved his family to California. Ira, a member of the Texas Ranger Hall of Fame, died of pneumonia at age 90, on August 5, 1953.

Albert Jennings Fountain mysteriously disappeared following his involvement in the Salt War. *Wild Horse Collection.*

Chapter Twenty-Four
Albert Jennings Fountain

Albert J. Fountain was born as Albert Jennings on Staten Island, New York, on October 23, 1838. His parents were Solomon Jennings, a sea captain, and Catherine de la Fontaine, a French Huguenot. While living in Sacramento, California as a young man, he adopted an Anglicized version of his mother's maiden name and henceforth would be known as Albert Jennings Fountain. Albert worked as a reporter for the Sacramento Union, freighted supplies to mining camps, and prospected for gold in his spare time. Later, Fountain studied law while working as an aide for Judge N. Greene Curtis. When the Civil War began, he joined the Union army by signing on with the First California Infantry Volunteers, better known as Carleton's California Column. His company was assigned to Fort Fillmore near Mesilla, New Mexico. At Mesilla, Albert met Mariana Perez and they were married on October 27, 1862. When the war ended Albert Fountain joined a militia group known as the Mesilla Scouts to help ward off the danger of Indian raids. In one conflict he received a nasty wound fighting Mescalero Apaches. Fountain soon moved Mariana and their two children to El Paso, Texas, to begin a career in law. The couple would eventually have ten more children.

Ben Dowell's saloon was a favorite meeting place for the political brass of El Paso. It was there that Albert met W. W. Mills, the Collector of Customs. Fountain tossed his hat into the political ring by running for, and winning the office of County Surveyor. Veterans of the Union army and Yankee sympathizers had a huge advantage during the days of Reconstruction. Following two other positions, Fountain was appointed Assessor and Collector of Internal Revenue for the Western District of Texas.

While employed as County Surveyor, San Antonio businessman Samuel A. Maverick recruited Fountain to survey the salt beds at the foot of Guadalupe Peak. Maverick claimed over one-half of the salt deposits in the area. Seeing a potential lucrative opportunity W. W. Mills, Fountain and others realized that there was plenty of salt outside of Maverick's boundaries. Furthermore, that they could sell it to the Hispanics, and others in the area. The organizers of the group that was known as the "Salt Ring" were W. W. Mills, A. J. Fountain, District Judge Gaylord Judd Clarke, A. H. French, B. F. Williams, and J. M. Lujan. It wasn't long before Mills and Fountain had a falling out. In fact, they attacked each other verbally and within political circles as much as possible. To the chagrin of Mills, Fountain was elected to the Texas State Senate. Now out of the "Salt Ring," one of the platforms on which Fountain ran his campaign was that he wanted to secure title to the salt deposits for the people of El Paso.

Tragedy struck on December 7, 1870. Though a member of the "Salt Ring," Judge Clarke had remained a friend of Fountain. The two were visiting at Ben Dowell's saloon when B. F. Williams, who obviously had too much to drink, approached and began tongue-lashing both Fountain and Clarke. Williams temper turned into rage, and he drew his pistol. Fountain was armed only with his cane, but he charged Williams anyway. B. F. Williams fired three shots at Fountain. All connected. One shot hit the Senator in the breast but was deflected by his watch, another grazed his head, and the third severed his left arm. Williams fled out the back door, and Fountain staggered to his house nearby. Albert Fountain wiped away his blood, grabbed his rifle, and despite the pleas of Mariana, he dashed back out into the street. Fountain fell in behind Judge Clarke and State Police Captain A. H. French who Clarke had fetched. They were on their way to Williams' place. B. F. Williams stepped through his door and at point blank range blasted Judge Clarke with a load of buckshot. The judge collapsed and died instantly. Albert Fountain immediately dropped Williams with a rifle shot. As Williams rolled over trying to reach his shotgun, Captain French fired a bullet into his head. Williams was dead.

Much bitter feeling followed the incident, and Fountain knew that his life was in danger. He avoided any more salt trouble, and when his term as senator was over, he moved his family from El Paso, back to Mesilla.

Just as he did in Texas, Fountain acquired political enemies in New Mexico. One was Albert Bacon Fall whom Fountain defeated in a race for a seat in the State House of Representatives in 1888. They ran against each other again in 1892 with Fall winning the seat. Their personal feud continued. In late January of 1896, Fountain traveled to Lincoln to present evidence against Oliver Lee, a friend of Fall, for cattle rustling. His eight-year-old son Henry accompanied him on the trip. On their 100-mile return trip on February 1st, they mysteriously disappeared as they crossed the White Sands desert. Blood stains were later found as well as the buggy containing Albert's cartridge belt and Henry's hat.

A stagecoach driver later testified that he passed Fountain's buggy, and that it was being followed by three men on horseback. Oliver Lee and Jim Gilliland were later tried for Henry's murder, but were acquitted. They were defended in the courtroom by Albert Fall.

On his deathbed, in 1949, Sam Ketchum informed authorities that his brother Tom had killed the Fountains and then burned the bodies. Tom "Blackjack" Ketchum was the leader of the infamous "Blackjack" Ketchum gang. He was decapitated by a hangman's noose as he dropped through the trapdoors in Clayton, New Mexico, on April 26, 1901. To substantiate his confession, Sam Ketchum, a gang member, produced the Masonic Lodge pin that Albert Fountain was wearing the day that he disappeared.

Judge Roy Bean is trying a horse thief at his saloon and courthouse in Langtry, Texas. *Texas State Library and Archives Commission.*

Chapter Twenty-Five
The Law West of the Pecos

One of the most colorful characters on the Texas frontier was Judge Roy Bean. So much legend is attributed to Bean that it is impossible to decipher between tall tales and truth (what there is of it). His saloon doubled as a courtroom where he tried many men that had been involved in gunfights. Bean would often recess a trial in order to sell his liquor.

Roy Bean was a native Kentuckian who found his way to Texas at an early age. He left a wife and children in San Antonio, and then drifted about the west working as a bartender and part time gambler. At some point, he connected with the Southern Pacific Railroad as it pushed westward. Bean established a tent saloon which he moved to keep pace with construction crews. When the railroad established a station at Langtry (which was named for an S.P.R. official, not Lily Langtry as Bean had claimed) his "portable" tent found a permanent location. Before long Roy Bean built a frame structure (14 ft. x 20 ft.) which was to be his courtroom, complete with a bar and poker tables. He hung out his shingle (several in fact) and proclaimed himself to be the "law west of the Pecos." As the nearest court was about 200 miles away, the Texas Rangers began bringing prisoners to Judge Bean, even before he was officially appointed as a justice of the peace.

Judge Roy Bean knew very little law, so he improvised. Wedding ceremonies usually ended with the pronouncement, "May God have mercy on your soul." When a federal judge advised Bean that he could perform marriages, but that divorces were not within the powers of a justice of the peace, Bean responded, "Well, I married them, so I reckon I have the right to rectify my errors."

Following an incident where a worker had fallen to his death from a viaduct, Bean (having pronounced the man dead) believed his $5 coroner's fee insufficient pay for his services. After discovering a revolver and $40 on the dead body, Bean proclaimed, "I find this corpse guilty of carrying a concealed weapon, so I fine it $40."

The Judge Roy Bean story most often told concerns an Irish railroad hand that had killed a Chinese worker. When the Irishman was hauled into court to face trial for murder, the courtroom was filled with his Irish buddies who were likely there to assure that he received a fair trial. Judge Bean surveyed the rough-looking crowd as he leafed through his statutes. Finally he proclaimed, "Although there are many prohibitions against homicide, there is no specific ban against killing a Chinese. This case is dismissed."

Roy Bean had an appreciation for the arts. He built an opera house which doubled as a town hall. Bean had a high regard for the theater, and an infatuation with actress Lily Langtry. He even named his saloon the Jersey Lilly (though his sign was misspelled) in her honor. In 1888, Bean traveled to San Antonio to watch the British actress perform on stage. It was the only time he saw the lady whom he admired so much.

With the exception of a two-year stint during which he was voted out of office, Judge Roy Bean tried cases for approximately twenty years until his death (from pneumonia) on March 19, 1903. He was seventy-eight years old when he died. For awhile he was the only judge between the Pecos River and El Paso. He did his thing—his way, and because of his unorthodox demeanor he etched his way into the annals of western history. He truly was (as he boasted) the "Law West of the Pecos."

Following his development of a mechanically revolving cylinder in 1835, Sam Colt became a leader in the production fo firearms. Colt has beene variously characterized as ambitious and demanding, yet personable and fair. *Colt's Manufacturing Company, Inc.*

Chapter Twenty-Six
Guns and Gun Makers

Repeating arms of one form or another date all the way back to the 16th Century, but even the flintlock pistols and longarms of the 18th Century had a high degree of unreliability. A major step occurred in the evolution of firearms when gun manufacturers moved from those inconsistent flintlocks to more dependable percussion caps. Samuel Colt revolutionized the manufacture of guns when he patented his revolver in England in 1835, and in the United States in 1836, and then mass produced it in both countries with advanced technological methods. Somebody once stated that "God created man, but Sam Colt made them equal!" Colt's handguns were among the most popular weapons used in the Old West.

In 1839, the government of Texas purchased 180 .36 caliber Paterson Colt revolvers from the Patent Arms Manufacturing Company, which were predominantly issued to the Rangers. Although the Patent Arms Manufacturing Company soon became defunct, the efficiency of Colt's revolvers had been established. With the assistance of Captain Samuel Walker, Colt was able to obtain a government contract (in 1847) for his .44 caliber Walker Colt revolver for use in the Mexican War. Eli Whitney Jr. manufactured the Walker Colt for Sam Colt. It was a heavy weapon – weighing over four and one-half pounds. Before long, Colt purchased Whitney's equipment and machinery and established his own manufacturing plant at Hartford, Connecticut. As the popularity of handguns increased, Colt produced a variety of different models.

Prior to 1849, much of the western frontier was a land of vast wilderness, sparsely inhabited by Indian tribes. White men who had previously ventured into the wilderness were, for the most part, trappers, fur traders or explorers. The discovery of gold (and later silver) was to change the face of the West dramatically. With dreams of riches, thousands of people migrated to the frontier by wagon, horseback or even on foot. They faced many perils in this little-known territory. The importance of carrying firearms was evident.

Various models of Sharps rifles and carbines were popular on the western frontier and during the Civil War. Although the muzzle-loading rifle's popularity remained strong for many years, the breech-loader had a distinct advantage in that it could be reloaded much more rapidly. After patenting his vertically sliding block design in 1848, Christian Sharps began production of a breech-loading single-shot rifle which was deemed to be highly accurate. During the years which followed, Sharps manufactured rifles up to .60 caliber. The .50 caliber Sharps rifle was a favorite of buffalo hunters. When Henry Ward Beecher was quoted in the New York Tribune in 1856 (in reference to Kansas slaveholders), he indicated that there was more moral power in Sharps rifles than in a hundred Bibles. Henceforth Sharps rifles were dubbed "Beecher's Bibles."

The first model produced by Horace Smith and Daniel Wesson (in 1857) was a seven-shot .22 caliber single-action handgun with a bored-through chamber. After realizing that Rollin White had patented such a chamber two years earlier, Smith & Wesson purchased his patent rights for cash and royalties. The White/Smith & Wesson patent rights were violated by several manufacturers. A couple of lawsuits were virtually ineffective and by late 1861 there were several handguns with bored-though chambers manufactured by competing firearms companies. The .22 caliber was hardly adequate on the western frontier, but Smith & Wesson quickly stepped up the size of their bore with a variety of new models. Smith & Wesson began producing (in 1861) a .32 caliber handgun, of which many eventually reached the western frontier. With a variety of new models, Smith & Wesson became one of the premiere handgun manufacturers. In 1854, a joint patent was issued with Smith & Wesson for a lever-action repeating pistol. It was the forerunner of the Volcanic rifles and pistols, the Henry rifle, and the extremely popular Winchester lever-action rifles. Smith & Wesson sold its rights to the lever-action, in 1855, to the Volcanic Repeating Arms Company, of which Oliver Winchester was a stockholder. Following the insolvency of Volcanic, the New Haven Arms Company was formed with Oliver Winchester as president and Benjamin Tyler Henry as plant superintendent. Henry obtained a patent, in 1860, on a level-action rifle with a rim fire cartridge design of his own. The Henry rifle was a predecessor of the farmed Winchester. Whereas the Spencer repeated rifle (patented by Christopher M. Spencer in 1860) was substantially more popular as a combat weapon during the Civil War, the Henry rifle achieved much success on the western frontier.

Pocket pistols (originally called pocket rifles) were also popular in the Old West. There was an ever-expanding market for weapons which could be easily concealed by hiding them in a pocket or elsewhere. Two famous manufacturers of pocket arms were Ethan Allen (who patented a self-cocking mechanism in 1837) and Henry Deringer, Jr.. Ethan Allen was on of the forerunners in the development of repeating handguns. Although Allen developed pistols with revolving barrels called "pepperboxes," Samuel Colt's design of revolving cylinders ultimately became more popular. Henry Deringer typically sold pocket pistols in pairs, usually in boxed sets. He so popularized the short-barreled single-shot pocket pistol that they became known as "Deringers." Many manufacturers (notably Colt, beginning in 1869) produced Deringers. Small pocket pistols were used for self-defense by both men and women and were a popular size for gamblers. Many men who used firearms to make their living (both lawmen and outlaws alike) relied on their Deringers as back-up weapons.

A significant development in the evolution of firearms was the advent of rimfire and centerfire cartridges. By about 1863, most of the more popular gun dealers in the Old West offered a wide range of firearms (both percussion and cartridge) of such manufacturers as Colt, Sharps, Smith & Wesson, and Remington. It was not until the early 1870s, however, that cartridge arms began to seriously threaten the dominance once held by percussion arms.

Although the metallic cartridge revolutionized the loading process, the use of black powder weapons was fairly common into the 1870s. Loading, or re-loading, was more complicated with muzzle-loading rifles and pistols. The weapon had to be held upright with its barrel pointed upwards. Black powder was poured directly into the chamber. Variations in the amount of powder used could have an effect on accuracy. A lead ball was seated on the chamber and then forced into the chamber by a ramrod or rammer. Obviously it was inconvenient to reload in this manner during battle or gunfight. Loading was considerably safer and more rapid using metallic cartridges.

In late 1864, the U.S. Army searched for a method to convert their thousands of muzzle-loading rifle-muskets to breechloaders. Erskine S. Allin of the Springfield Armory solved the dilemma when he patented his conversion method in September of 1865. The Model 1865 Springfield, otherwise known as "Allin's Alteration," or the "needle gun," was the first government conversion. The Model 1866 Springfield, with the new Allin design, was even more efficient. Through about 1873, the Springfield remained the preferred infantry rifle, especially the Model 1870. Where mounted troops were concerned the seven-shot Spencer carbine was used predominately in the cavalry's postwar Indian fighting. The Springfield No. 99 (the .45-.70s of 1873) soon became the standard weapon for both U.S. infantry and cavalry. It remained so for many years. In 1886, the French developed a small-caliber, high-velocity cartridge with "smokeless powder," an innovation which was to have a profound effect on firearms worldwide. This, coupled with the production of new reliable repeating rifles, eventually rendered the trapdoor Springfield obsolete.

As greater numbers of settlers pushed westward, violence on the frontier increased, as well. Whereas Indians and wild animals once posed the greatest threat to pioneers, clashes between white men occurred at an increasing rate. Some of the hostilities grew out of the Civil War, while others were the result of growing conflicts between the lawful and the lawless. In a land where judges and lawmen were scarce, frontiersmen often chose to take justice into their own hands. Self-preservation was often determined by the ability of a man to use his firearms, as well as the efficiency of those weapons.

During the 1850s and 60s the most popular handguns on the frontier were the Model 1851 Navy and Model 1860 Army Colts, and the Remington New Models. The Colt and Remington .44s were extremely

The Colt Single-Action Army was introduced in 1873. Commonly known as the "Peacemaker," this solid-fram, six-shot revolver became the most popular handgun on the western frontier. *Wild Horse Collection.*

popular in the western civilian market. Between 1867 and 1872, Colt remained busy converting cap and ball revolvers to use metallic cartridges and therefore did not produce an original metallic cartridge revolver until 1873. Colt introduced its Single-Action Army revolver in 1873. The new model had a solid frame, and a six-shot cylinder which opened to the side featuring a side-rod ejector. It was initially chambered for a new .45 caliber center fire cartridge. The Colt Single-Action Army, more commonly known as the Peacemaker, was destined to become the most famous handgun of its era. The U.S. government issued an initial contract to Colt for 8,000 units. The Peacemaker made an immediate impression on the civilian market, as well, because it was rugged, easy to handle, would cock rapidly and had excellent handling qualities.

In 1870, Smith & Wesson introduced their Model 3, the first large bore (.44 caliber) metallic cartridge revolver to be manufactured. Its innovative extractor ejected the previously fired shells when the handgun was opened for reloading. The extractor reduced reloading time by nearly one-half. This feature made the handgun a favorite of many outlaws – including Jesse James. The Model 3 was redesigned by Major George W. Schofield of the Tenth Cavalry and the Schofield name became an integral part of ensuing Smith & Wesson models.

By 1873 the four major American firearms manufacturers were Colt, Remington, Smith & Wesson and Winchester. Colt was still manufacturing a few revolving rifles but would shortly discontinue them. They also manufactured shotguns, lever-action rifles and slide-action rifles. Because of their inability to compete with the more successful shoulder arms of Winchester, Colt eventually abandoned these lines in order to concentrate on their highly successful handguns. Remington manufactured shotguns, rifles and pistols. During the late 1860s, Remington had popularized its famed rolling-block design on rifles and carbines. The rolling-block action was also used on the Remington Model 1871 .50 caliber single-shot pistol. Smith & Wesson, producers of a few rifles and lever-action pistols during its earlier years, turned its attention to specifically manufactured revolvers. Although Oliver Winchester had limited success with the Henry rifle, his greatest success would come from the rifle which was to bear his name – Winchester. The company which originally was the New Haven Arms Company, changed its name to the Henry Repeating Rifle Company and then changed again (in 1866) to become the Winchester Repeating Arms Company.

Winchester's superintendent, Nelson King, patented a revolutionary new magazine tube in May of 1866. King's magazine could be loaded with fifteen cartridges. To load the rifle, cartridges were simply pushed through a spring tempered loading gate located in the right side of the receiver. It was incorporated into the first rifle to bear Winchester's name – the Model 1866. A brass receiver was added to the weapon which otherwise was very similar to its predecessor, the Henry. The Model 1866 was also available as a carbine. A few years later, the legendary Winchester Model 1873 was introduced. The new model boasted a center fire .44-40 cartridge (.44 caliber plus 40 grains of powder) and an iron receiver. The Model 1873 (produced continuously until 1919) was widely popular in the civilian market. The Winchester Model 1876 was slightly modified to receive .45-70 or .45-75 cartridges. The brilliant innovator and patent-master, John M. Browning, developed the Model 1886 Winchester. It was smoother, stronger and superior to any Winchester previously manufactured. The Model 1886 could handle the .45-70 and various other calibers. The popular "86" was sold by gun dealers all over the Old West. Other successful Browning inspired Winchesters were the Model 1892, Model 1894 and Model 1895.

By the late 1880s the Winchester lever-action had only one major competitor – Marlin. John Marlin's Model 1889 introduced a solid-op, side-ejection receiver through which fired shells ejected from the upper right of the receiver. Further modification resulted in the Model 1893 which was designed to handle long cartridges such as the .32-40. The 1889 and 1893 were two of Marlin's most popular models. Arthur Savage marketed a new hammerless lever-action repeater with his .303 caliber Savage Model 1896. It sold well, as did the Savage Model 1899, but the Savage Repeating Arms Company never experienced the success of either Winchester or, to a lesser degree, Marlin. Although the competition offered some fine products, Winchester rifles and carbines remained, by far, the most popular in the West.

In 1869, at the age of fourteen, John Moses Browning completely assembled a slide rifle from spare parts. Nine years later he created his first gun, a breech loading single-shot rifle. The production rights to Browning's first rifle were purchased by Winchester. The gun became the Winchester Model 1885 High Wall and would be the first of 44 Browning designs purchased by Winchester. More than 80 separate firearms developed from 128 Browning patents. He was truly the greatest gun inventor of all time. In addition to Winchester, he was responsible for

The Winchester Model 1892 lever-action repeating rifle was manufactured in calibers of .44-40, .38-40, .32-20, and .25-20. *Wild Horse Collection.*

The J. M. Browning & Brothers factory and store, Ogden, Utah Territory, about 1882. Not the mis-spelling of the word ammunition. Shown left to right are Sam Browning, George Browning, John Moses Browning, Mathew Browning, Ed Browning and Frank Rushton. *Browning.*

the gun designs of many manufacturers – including Remington, Colt, Fabrique Nationale (Belgium), Browning, Savage, Stevens, Ithaca and the U.S. Military.

Shotguns played an important role in firearms of the Old West. Not only was the shotgun used for hunting, but it was the preferred weapon for many when a gunfight was inevitable. Stagecoach drivers were usually equipped with pistols and shotguns. Wells Fargo messengers often carried sawed-off shotguns. Doc Holliday's favorite weapon was a double-barrel shotgun. Brothers Charles and John Parker began manufacturing one of the more popular shotguns in 1867. Parker shotguns were available in 10, 11 and 12-gauge. Their advertisements, which were seen in many western newspapers, advertised Parker shotguns from $50 to about $200 for a well-adorned version. Remington also made inroads into the western market. Its models were competitively priced with the Parker. Although they never rivaled the dominance of Parker and Remington, Stevens and Colt entered the shotgun market in 1877 and 1878 respectively. Both offered 10 and 12-gauge barrels. Harrington & Richardson introduced a hammerless double in 1883. Ithaca and L.C. Smith successfully manufactured shotguns, as well. A lever-action shotgun, a product of the ingenious John M. Browning, was introduced by Winchester in 1887. The Model 1887 was also available in both 10 and 12-gauge. Winchester began marketing another browning invention in 1893 – a pump shotgun. A perfected version of the M1893, Winchester's Model 1897, became one of the best selling repeating shotguns ever produced.

Our Constitution gives each individual the "right to bear arms." Most Americans interpret those words to mean the right to possess firearms for use in defending one's home, property, family or self. Since the days of the Revolutionary War, we have been a gun-owning society. Through the years gun makers have provided a wide variety of models from which an individual might choose – and choose we have. The "right to bear arms" was probably never more evident than during the days of the so-called lawless Old West, where many individuals felt the necessity to carry weapons with them at all times

BOOKS

Adams, Ramon F. *Six-Guns & Saddle Leather: A Bibliography of Books & Pamphlets on Western Outlaws and Gunmen*. Norman: University of Oklahoma Press, 1969.

Bartholomew, Ed. *Black Jack Ketchum: Last of the Hold-Up Kings*. Houston: Frontier Press of Texas, 1955.

Block, Eugene B. *Great Train Robberies of the West*. New York: Coward-McCann, Inc., 1959.

Breihan, Carl W. *Great Lawmen of the West*. New York: Bonanza Books, 1963.

Breihan, Carl W. *Ride the Razor's Edge*. Gretna, LA: Pelican Publishing Co., 1992.

Brown, John Henry. *History of Texas, from 1685 to 1892. Volume One*. St. Louis, MO: Beckktold & Co., 1892.

Burton, Jeff. *Dynamite and Six-shooter*. Santa Fe: Palomino Press, 1970.

Calvert, Robert A. and Arnoldo De Leon. *The History of Texas. Second Edition*. Wheeling, IL: Harlan Davidson, Inc., 1996.

Castleman, Harvey N. *Sam Bass: The Train Robber*. Girard, Ks: Haldeman-Julius Publications, 1944.

Chamblin, Thomas S., ed. *The Historical Encyclopedia of Texas*. Austin: The Texas Historical Institute, 1982.

Chrisman, Harry E. *The Ladder of Rivers*. Denver: Sage Books, 1962.

Coe, George W. *Frontier Fighter*. Albuquerque: University of New Mexico Press, 1934.

Coolidge, Dane. *Fighting Men of the West*. New York: E.P. Dutton, 1932.

Cox, William R. *Luke Short and His Era*. Garden City, NY: Doubleday and Co., Inc., 1961.

Elman, Robert. *Badmen of the West*. Scaucus, NJ: Ridge Press, Inc., 1974.

Erwin, Allen A. *The Southwest of John H. Slaughter, 1841-1922: Pioneer Cattleman and Traildriver of Texas, the Pecos, and Arizona and Sheriff of Tombstone.* Glendale, CA: Arthur II. Clark Co., 1965.

Ewell, Thomas T. *History of Hood County.* Granbury, TX: Frank Gaston, Publisher, 1895. Reprinted by the Junior Woman's Club, Granbury, TX, 1956.

Fehrenbach, T.R. Lone Star: A History of Texas and the Texans. New York: Collier Books, 1985.

Fisher, O.c, and J.C Dykes. *King Fisher: His Life and Times.* Norman: University of Oklahoma Press, 1960.

Garavaglia, Louis A. and Charles G. Worman. *Firearms of the American West, 1803-1865.* Albuquerque: University of New Mexico Press, 1984.

Garavaglia, Louis A. and Charles G. Worman. *Firearms of the American West, 1866-1894.* Albuquerque: University of New Mexico Press, 1985.

Gard, Wayne. *Frontier Justice.* Norman: University of Oklahoma Press, 1949.

Gard, Wayne. *Sam Bass.* Boston and New York: Houghton Mifflin, 1936.

Hall, Sarah Harkey. *Surviving on the Texas Frontier.* Austin: Eakin Press, 1996.

Hardin, John Wesley. *The Life of John Wesley Hardin as Written by Himself.* Norman: University of Oklahoma Press, 1961.

Harkey, Dee. *Mean as Hell.* Santa Fe, NM: Ancient City Press, 1989.

Horan, James D. *The Authentic Wild West: The Gunfighters.* New York: Crown Publishers, Inc., 1976.

Hunter, J. Marvin and Noah H. Rose. *The Album of Gunfighters.* San Antonio: Hunter and Rose, 1951.

Jahns, Pat. *The Frontier World of Doc Holliday.* New York: Hastings House, 1957.

James, Vinton Lee. *Frontier and Pioneer Recollections of Early Days in San Antonio and West Texas.* San Antonio: Vinton Lee James, 1938.

Jennings, N.A. *A Texas Ranger.* New York: Charles Scribner's Sons, 1899.

Lamar, Howard R. (Ed.). *The Reader's Encyclopedia of the American West.* New York: Thomas Y. Crowell Co., 1977.

Llewellyn, Karl N., and E. Adamson Hoebel. *The Cheyenne Way: Conflict and Case Law in Primitive Jurisprudence.* Norman: University of Oklahoma Press, 1941.

Malone, Dumas, ed. *Dictionary of American Biography.* New York: Charles Scribner's Sons, 1943.

Metz, Leon C. *Dallas Stoudenmire.* Norman: Universirty of Oklahoma Press, 1979.

Metz, Leon C. *John Selman, Gunfighter.* Norman: University of Oklahoma Press, 1980.

Moody, Ralph. *Stagecoach West.* New York: Thomas Y. Crowell Co., 1967.

Nash, Jay Robert. *Encyclopedia of Western Lawmen & Outlaws.* New York: Paragon House, 1992.

Nolan, Frederick. *Bad Blood: The Life and Times of the Horrell Brothers.* Stillwater, OK: Barbed Wire Press, 1994.

Nordyke, Lewis. *John Wesley Hardin: Texas Gunman.* New York: William Morrow & Co., 1957.

Olmstead, Frederick Law. *A Journey Through Texas; or, a Saddle-trip on the Southwestern Frontier: with a Statistical Appendix.* New York: Dix, Edwards and Co., 1857.

O'Neal, Bill. *Encyclopedia of Western Gunfighters.* Norman: University of Oklahoma Press, 1979.

Paine, Lauran. *Texas Ben Thompson.* Los Angeles: Westernlore Press, 1966.

Parsons, Chuck. *Clay Allison: Portrait of a Shootist.* Seagraves, TX, Pioneer Book Publishers, 1983.

Parsons, Chuck. *Robert Clay Allison: Gentleman Gunfighter.* Pecos TX, West of the Pecos Museum Press, 1977.

Polk, Stella Gipson. *Mason and Mason County: A History.* Austin: The Pemberton Press, 1966.

Prassel, Frank Richard. *The Western Peace Officer: A Legacy of Law and Order*. Norman: University of Oklahoma Press, 1972.

Preece, Harold. *Lone Star Man—Ira Aten*. New York: Hastings House, 1960.

Rathmell, William (Edited by). *Life of the Marlows, A True Story of Frontier Life of Early Days*. University of North Texas Press, 1984.

Rennert, Vincent Paul. *Western Outlaws*. New York: Crowell-Collier Press, 1968.

Robinson, Charles. *The Men Who Wear the Star: The Story of the Texas Rangers*. New York: Random House, 2000.

Rosa, Joseph G. *Age of the Gunfighter: Men and Weapons on the Frontier 1840-1900*. Norman: University of Oklahoma Press, 1995.

Rose, Victor M. *The Texas Vendetta; or, The Sutton-Taylor Feud*. New York: J. J. Little and Co., 1956.

San Saba Historical Commission. *San Saba County History: 1856-1983*. San Angelo, TX: News Foto, 1983.

Secrest, William B. *Lawmen & Desperadoes*. Spokane: The Arthur H. Clark Company, 1994.

Sonnichsen, C.L. *I'll Die Before I'll Run*. New York: The Devin-Adair Co., 1962.

Sonnichsen, C.L. Outlaw. *Bill Mitchell alias Baldy Russell*. His Life and Times. Denver: Sage Books, 1965.

Stanley, F. *Clay Allison*. Denver: World Press, Inc., 1956.

Stanley, F. *Jim Courtright: Two Gun Marshal of Fort Worth*. Denver: World Press, Inc., 1957.

Steckmesser, Kent Ladd. *The Western Hero in History and Legend*. Norman: University of Oklahoma Press, 1965.

Stephens, Robert W. *Texas Ranger Sketches*. Dallas: Self-published, 1972.

Stiles, T.J. *In Their Own Words: Warriors and Pioneers*. New York: The Berkley Publishing Group, 1996.

Sreeter, Floyd B. *Ben Thompson: Man With A Gun*. New York: Frederick Fell, Inc., 1957.

Summerfield, Charles. [Alfred W. Arrington]. *The Desperadoes of the Southwest: containing an account of the Cane-Hill murders, together with the lives of several of the most notorious regulators and moderators of that region,* New York: W.H. Graham, 1847.

Sutton, Fred Ellsworth. *Hands Up!: Stories of the Six-Gun Fighters of the Old Wild West.* As told to A.B. McDonald. Indianapolis: Bobbs-Merrill, 1927.

Sutton, Robert C., Jr. *The Sutton-Taylor Feud.* Quanah, TX: Nortex Press, 1974.

Tanner, Karen Holliday. *Doc Holliday: A Family Portrait.* Norman: University of Oklahoma Press, 1998.

Thrapp, Dan L. *Encyclopedia of Frontier Biography: Vols I, II, III, IV.* Lincoln: University of Nebraska Press, 1988.

Trachtman, Paul. ed. *The Gunfighters.* New York: Time-Life Books, 1974.

U.S. Bureau of the Census, Revised by the Social Science Research Council. *The Statistical History of the United States from Colonial Times to the Present.* Stanford: Fairfield Publishers, Inc., 1965.

Webb, Walter Prescott. *The Texas Rangers: A Century of Frontier Defense.* Austin, University of Texas Press, 1965.

Wellman, Paul I. *A Dynasty of Western Outlaws.* Lincoln, NE: The University of Nebraska Press, 1985.

Wilkins, Frederick. *The Legend Begins: The Texas Rangers, 1823-1845.* Austin: State House Press, 1996.

NEWSPAPERS

Albuquerque Review
Austin Statesman
Austin American Statesman
Austin Tribune
Bastrop Advertiser
Dallas Morning News
Dallas Times-Herald
Houston Chronicle
Houston Daily Post
Houston Post
Laredo Daily Times
Oklahoma State Capital (Oklahoma City, OK)
Tombstone Epitaph

ARTICLES

Adams, Paul. "The Unsolved Murder of Ben Thompson, Pistoleer Extraordinary," Southwestern Historical Quarterly, Vol. XLVII, No. 3 (January 1945), 321-29.

Berrier, Deborah. "Clay Allison Never Killed a Man Willingly." American History Illustrated, Summer, 1982.

Berrier, Deborah. "Clay Allison: Shootist." American History Illustrated 1982 17(4): 38-39.

Carlson, Paul H. "Panhandle Pastores: Early Sheepherding in the Texas Panhandle." Panhandle-Plains Historical Review 1980. 53: 1-15.

Cawelti, John G. "The Gunfighter and Society," The American West, Vol. V, No. 2 (March 1968), 30-35, 76-78.
Holden, W. C. "Law and Lawlessness on the Texas Frontier, 1875-1890," Southwestern Historical Quarterly, Vol. XLIV, No. 2 (October 1940), 188-203.

Koop, Waldo E., "Enter John Wesley Hardin, A Dim Trail to Abilene." The Prairie Scout, Vol. II, ed. by The Westerners. Ives Printing Co., 1974.

McGinty, Brian. "John Wesley Hardin: Gentleman of Guns." American History Illustrated, Summer 1982.

Robbins, Peggy. "Sam Bass: The Texas Robin Hood." American History Illustrated, 1982 17(4): 37.

Rohrs, Richard C. "The Study of Oklahoma History During the Territorial Period: An Alternative Methodological Approach." Chronicles of Oklahoma, 1982 60(2): 174-185.

Weiss, Harold J., Jr. "Western Lawmen: Image and Reality." Journal of the West, 1985 24(1): 23-32.

Wharton, Clarence. "Early Judicial History of Texas," Texas Law Review, Vol. XII, No. 3 (April 1934), 311-25.

OTHER SOURCES

Austin History Center

Austin Public Library

Criminal Dockets, First Judicial District, New Mexico Territory, August 1, 1882-March 26, 1912.

Federal Records Center, Denver, CO:

G. R. Fardon Photo Files.

George Eastman House Collection.

Hubbs Enterprises, Pecos, TX: Barney Hubbs Collection, Clay Allison Files.

McCubbin, Robert G. Collection, El Paso, TX.

Oklahoma Historical Society, Oklahoma City, OK: Foreman, Grant -- U.S. Marshal, Vertical File. Indian-Pioneer History (W.P.A. Project, 1937).

University of Texas at Austin, The Dolph Briscoe Center for American History, Special Collections.

United States Geological Survey, Maps, U.S. Department of the Interior, Federal Center, Denver.

Wild Horse Collection, Round Rock, TX.

Index

A

Abilene, Kansas 19, 21
Acme Saloon 23
Ada, Oklahoma 67, 68
Albuquerque, Texas 83
Allen, Ethan 149
Allin, Erskine S. 150
Allison, John 40
Allison, Robert Clay 39, 40
Appomattox, Virginia 45
Armstrong, John 22
Arnold, Mace "Winchester Smith" 89
Aten, Imogen Boyce 139
Aten, Ira 58, 60, 137 - 139
Austin, Texas 22, 99

B

Baker, Cullen Montgomery 93, 94, 96
Bank's Saloon and Billiard Parlor 81, 82
Barnes, Seaborn 41 - 43
Barrickman, Alec 85, 86
Bass, Sam 6, 41 - 43, 134, 137
Battle of the Alamo 6
Bean, Roy (Judge) 7, 145, 146
Beard, Mose 63, 64
Beatty, Az 118
Beatty, Jack 118
Beavers, Jim 10
Bell County, Texas 97, 107 - 109
Bell, C. S. (Captain) 71, 72, 80
Big Springs, Nebraska 41
Bishop, Thomas 117, 118
Blakely, Jake 56, 59
Bobbitt, Gus 68
Bonham, Texas 19, 46
Boren, Bill 48
Boren, Henry 48
Botas, the 129 - 131
Bowen, Bill 26, 27, 30 - 32
Brahma Bull and Red Hot Bar 56 - 58
Browning, John Moses 152, 153
Burkhart, William D. 11, 12

C

Camp Brown, Wyoming 96, 97
Camp King, Texas 137
Canadian, Texas 123
Carlsbad, New Mexico (formerly Eddy, New Mexico) 51, 52
Chisholm Trail 43, 137
Choate, Crockett 71, 76, 77
Choate, John 71, 73, 74, 76, 77
Christian, Hiram (Judge) 107 - 109
Civil War, the (the War Between the States) 6, 13, 25, 45, 46, 61, 70, 93, 103, 107, 111, 129, 130, 134, 141, 148 - 150
Clark, Dr. Calvin 107, 109
Clarke, Gaylord Judd (District Judge) 142
Clark, Elijah 47
Clements, Emmanuel "Mannen" 21, 23, 82
Clements, Sallie 23
Clift, Louis 11, 12
Clinton, Texas 78, 82 - 84, 86, 89
Collier, Thomas B. "Tom" (Deputy Sheriff) 10, 11
Colt, Sam 147, 148
Comanche Indians 115
Comanche, Texas 22, 61, 85, 86, 91, 115
Cooley, Scott 62 - 65
Cortinas, Juan 6
Courtright, Jim (Timothy Isaiah Courtright) 6, 13 - 17
Coy, Jacob 100
Craddock, Billy 116
Crumpton, Zachariah 27, 28, 30
Cuero, Texas 78, 81, 82, 84, 85, 89
Cummings, Doc 104, 105

D

Dallas Times-Herald 127
Davis, Edmund J. (Governor) 26, 77 - 80
Day, Alfred Hays 81
Denton, Texas 41 - 43
Deringer, Henry Jr. 149
Derrickson, John E. 10
DeWitt County, Texas 71 - 73, 75, 78 - 80, 84 - 86, 90
Dixon, Bill 22
Dixon, Billy 47
Dodge City, Kansas 15
Dry Creek 9 - 12

E

Early, John 107 - 109
Earp, Wyatt 15
Eddy, New Mexico. *See* Carlsbad, New Mexico
El Paso, Texas 23, 30, 103 - 105, 141 - 143, 146
El Reno, Oklahoma 122, 123
Erhart, Pat 117
Estabo, Tranquellano 52, 53
Evergreen, Texas 96

F

Faber, Charles (Deputy Sheriff) 40
Fall, Albert Bacon 143
Fence Cutting War of 1886 138
Fisher, John King 99 - 101
Fort Bend County, Texas 55 - 58, 60, 137, 139
Fort Mason, Texas 61 - 71
Fort Sill, Oklahoma 10
Fort Stanton, New Mexico 28, 113
Fort Worth, Texas 14 - 16, 158
Foster, Joe 99, 100
Fountain, Albert Jennings 6, 141, 143
Fountain, Henry 143
Fountain, Mariana Perez 141
Frazer, G. A. "Bud" 67, 68
French, A. H. 142
Frost, H. H. 56 - 59

G

Garvey, Jim (Sheriff) 56, 58
Gibson, Ned 57, 60
Gibson, Volney 55 - 60
Giddings, Marsh (Governor) 28
Giddings, Texas 95, 97
Gladden, George 63, 64
Gonzales, Dario 129, 130
Gonzales Enquirer 84
Graham, Texas 10, 11
Griffin, David 109
Grimes, A. W. (Deputy Sheriff) 42, 43
Guaraches, the 129 - 131
Gylam, Jacob L. "Jack" (Sheriff) 27, 28

H

Hamilton, Andrew J. (Governor) 134

Harbolt, George E. 10
Harbolt, Susan 10
Hardin, Jane Bowen 21
Hardin, Joe 85, 86
Hardin, John Wesley "Wes" 19 - 24, 82, 83, 85, 86Harkey, D. R. "Dee" 49 - 54
Harkey, Joe 50, 51
Harkey, Sophie New 49, 51
Harrell, George (Texas Ranger) 43
Harris, Jack 99, 100
Hart, Edward "Little" 29, 30
Hash Knife Ranch 54
Hasley, Sam 107 - 109
Haynes, J. J. 129
Hays, John C. 133
Helm, Jack 22, 71 - 76, 78 - 80, 82, 83
Henry, Benjamin Tyler 149
Hickok, James Butler "Wild Bill" 13, 21
Higgins, John Calhoun Pinckney "Pink" 31 - 33, 36, 37
Hoerster, Dan 63
Holstein, Sim 80, 81
Holston, James H. 9
Hoodoo War, the (the Mason County War) 37, 61 - 65
Horrell, Ben 27 - 29
Horrell-Higgins Feud 25, 31 - 37
Horrell, Mart 25-36
Horrell, Merritt 29 - 31
Horrell, Sam Jr. 25 - 36
Horrell, Tom 25 - 36
Horrell War, the 25, 27 - 30
Houston, Laura Cross 121
Houston, Margaret Moffette (Lea) 121
Houston, Sam 121
Houston Telegraph 84
Houston, Temple Lea 121 - 127
Hudson, Dick (Deputy Sheriff) 89
Hudson, Hugh 46
Hughes, John R. 138
Hunter, Kit 89

I

Indianola, Texas 70, 85, 87 - 91
Indian Territory 10

J

Jackson, Frank 41 - 43

Jaybirds, the 55 - 60, 139
Jaybird-Woodpecker Conflict, the 55 - 60, 139
Jennings, Al 126
Jennings, Ed 125, 126
Jennings, John 125, 126
Johnson, Andrew (President) 45
Johnson, Bill 104
Johnson, Dick 48
Johnson, Jake 15
Jones, John B. (Major) 33, 34, 37, 64, 65

K

Ketchum, Samuel W. "Sam" 143
Ketchum, Thomas Edward "Black Jack" 143
King, Martin 89

L

Lackey, John 21
Lake Valley, New Mexico 14
Lampasas, Texas 25, 26, 30 - 34, 36, 42, 50
Langtry, Texas 145, 146
Laredo, Texas 129, 131, 138
Las Animas, Colorado 39
Las Cruces, New Mexico 25
Leadville, Colorado 15
Leavenworth, Kansas 96
Lee, Bob 45 - 48
Lee-Peacock Feud 45 - 48
Lee, Robert E. (General) 45, 69
Lexington, Texas 96, 116
Life of John Wesley Hardin as Written by Himself 23, 156
Lincoln, New Mexico 25, 27, 113
Little Rock, Arkansas 13
Logan, John "Black Jack" (General) 13 - 15
Long Branch Saloon 15
Longley, Cale 97
Longley, Wliam Preston "Bill" 6, 95 - 97

M

Maddox, Francis 45
Maddox, John 45
Maddox, William 45
Madsen, Chris (Deputy U. S. Marshal) 123
Manning, Doc 105
Manning, Frank 104, 105
Manning, Jim 105

Manning, John 105
Marlow, Alfred 9 - 12
Marlow, Boone 9 - 11
Marlow, Charles 9 - 12
Marlow, George 9 - 12
Marlow, Lewellyn "Ep" 9 - 12
Martin, Raymond 129, 130
Mason, Texas 61
Masterson, William Barclay "Bat" 15, 122
Matagorda Bay 88
Maverick, Samuel A. 142
McClelland, Andrew 139
McClelland, Hugh 139
McDade, Texas 115 - 118
McIntire, Jim 14, 15
McNelly, Leander H. (Captain) 86, 90
McRae, Jim 108, 109
Mescalero Apaches 141
Mesilla Scouts 141
Mexican War 6, 148
Miller, "Deacon" Jim 6, 23, 49, 67, 68
Mills, Alexander H. "Ham" (Sheriff) 28
Mills, W. W. 142
Milmo, Daniel 129
Milmo, Patricio 129
Milton, George 117, 118
Milton, Jeff Davis (Chief) 23
Mitchell, Nelson "Cooney" 111 - 114
Mitchell, Robert "Bob" 31 - 34, 37
Mitchell, William Nelson "Bill" 111 - 114, 158
Mobeetie, Texas 121, 122
Montaño, José 28
Morose, Helen Buelah 23
Morose, Martin 23
Morton, W. H. (Deputy U. S. Marshal) 12
Murphy, Jim 41 - 43

N

Nation, Carry 56
Nite, Jim 53, 54
Notch Cutters 115 - 117, 119

O

Oakwood Cemetery 16, 17
Oklahoma State Capital 127, 159
Olive Ranch 116

Olympic Dance Hall 40
Outlaw, Bass (Deputy U. S. Marshal) 23, 139

P

Paddleford, Walter 53
Parker, James Wesson (Judge) 56, 59
Parker, Joe 48
Patrón, Juan 28, 29
Peacock, Lewis 46 - 48
Pecos, Texas 40
Pensacola, Florida 22, 90
Pett's Ferry 94
Phoenix, New Mexico 51 - 53
Pierce, A. H. "Shanghai" 71
Pierce, Dr. William 46
Pilot Grove, Texas 46
Pleasant Valley War 54
Pridgen, Bolivar 79, 84 - 86, 91
Pridgen, Jim 84
Pridgen, Wiley 84

Q

Quantrill, William Clark 31, 48
Quillin, Mollie 122
Quinn, Mary 51

R

Randlett, James (Captain) 30
Reconstruction Acts 69
Regulator-Moderator War 6
Remington Firearms 149 - 151, 153
Republic of Texas 133
Reynolds, J. J. (General) 47
Richland Springs, Texas 49, 51
Richmond, John 14
Richmond, Texas 55, 60, 139
Rio Grande River 130, 134, 137
Rio Hondo 29
Roberts, Judd 138
Rock Island Railroad 53
Rock Saloon 115, 118
Ross, Lawrence S. (Governor) 59, 139
Roswell, New Mexico 29
Round Rock, Texas 41 - 43, 137

S

St. Joseph, Missouri 96
Salt Ring 142
San Antonio, Texas 50, 70, 71, 80, 99, 100, 109, 113, 138, 142, 145, 146
San Augustin Church 129
San Augustin Plaza 129
San Saba County, Texas 6, 49, 50
Savage, Arthur 152
Scarborough, George (Deputy U. S. Marshal) 23
Scott, Jerry 26 - 28, 30, 31
Selman, John 23, 157
Selman, Jr., John 23
Shackelford County, Texas 6
Sharps, Christian 148
Shelby County, Texas 6
Short, Luke Lamar 13 - 17
Silver City, New Mexico 14, 15
Simms, Billy 99, 100
Skidmore, F. O. 71, 75
Slaughter, Gabriel 85, 91
Smith, Martin (Parson) 46
Smith, Van C. 29, 30
Smith & Wesson 148, 149, 151
Son, Alfred 123 - 125
Southern Pacific Railroad 145
Spencer, Christopher M. 149
Stoudenmire, Dallas 103 - 105, 157
Sutton, Bill 78 - 87, 89 - 91
Sutton, Laura 83, 85, 87

T

Tascosa, Texas 122
Taylor, Amanda 78, 79
Taylor, Bill 85, 88 - 91
Taylor, Charley 78, 79
Taylor, Creed 69, 70, 72 - 75
Taylor, Hays 70, 71, 74
Taylor, Jim 22, 81, 83, 85 - 89
Taylor, Phillip "Doboy" 70, 72, 78, 80
Taylor, Pitkin 78 - 81
Taylor, Susan Cochran Day 78
Taylor, William Riley Jr. "Buck" 71, 78
Terry, Kyle 57, 60
Terry, Will 139
Texas Central Railroad 115

Texas Rangers 14, 22, 31, 33, 37, 42, 58, 59, 62 - 65, 68, 78, 86, 90, 104, 133 - 135, 137 - 139, 145
Texas Rangers' Frontier Battalion 33, 37
Texas State Legislature 122
Texas State Police 20, 21, 26, 27, 31, 78 - 80, 134, 142
Texas Supreme Court 130
Thompson, Ben 99, 100, 157
T.I.C. Commercial Detective Agency 15
Tombstone, Arizona 15, 30
Truitt, Jim (Reverend) 113, 114
Tucker, Tom 54
Turner Hall Opera House 100

U

Union League 45, 46
Ute Indians 97

V

Vaudeville Theatre and Gambling Saloon 99, 100
Vaughan, J. F. 36

W

Waco, Texas 20, 36, 82
Wallace, Marion DeKalb (Sheriff) 10, 11
Ware, Dick (Texas Ranger) 42, 43
Webb, Charles (Deputy Sheriff) 22, 85, 86, 91
Weeks, Sarah Elizabeth "Betty" 14
Weightman, George "Red Buck" 124
White Elephant Saloon 15
Wilburn, Aaron 30
Williamson, Tim 62, 63
Winchester, Oliver 149, 151
Winchester Repeating Arms Company 148, 149, 151 - 154
Woodpeckers, the 55 - 60
Worley, John (Deputy Sheriff) 62, 63
Wren, Wlliam "Bill" 31, 32
Wynn, Allen 117, 118

X

XIT Ranch 139

Y

Yavapai County, Arizona 30
Yorktown, Texas 72, 74, 75, 96

www.ingramcontent.com/pod-product-compliance
Lightning Source LLC
Chambersburg PA
CBHW071453080526
44587CB00014B/2092